Canopy of Refuge

Canopy of Refuge

Thoughts from Above

FRANK L. JOHNSON, III

Pleasant Word (a division of WinePress Publishing, PO Box 428, Enumclaw, WA 98022) functions only as book publisher. As such, the ultimate design, content, editorial accuracy, and views expressed or implied in this work are those of the author.

ISBN 1-4141-0761-7
Library of Congress Catalog Card Number: 2006904451

Dedication

I would first, like to dedicate this book to the only One who could have made this possible—God! Without Him, I would never have been able to write this book.

I would also like to dedicate this book to my wife of 17 years, Jean Johnson, and to my seven-year-old daughter, Miranda Lynne Johnson.

I could never leave out my dad, Francis Leo Johnson, Jr. and my mom, Patricia Johnson.

> The LORD also will be a refuge for the oppressed,
> A refuge in times of trouble.
> And those who know Your name will put their trust in You;
> For You, LORD, have not forsaken those who seek You.
>
> —Psalm 9:9-10

Table of Contents

Acknowledgements

This book would not have been possible four years ago. I was lost, going to hell, and didn't even know it. However, *God* intervened! *He* spoke to my heart and saved me for eternity on October 7, 2001.

I thank our friends James and Kathy Fry for inviting us to Second Baptist Church. I heard a man preaching that day, a man I had never met. *God* used and spoke through him in a mighty way. The words he spoke were not his words, but words directly from *God*. It was as if *God* was speaking directly to me. I thank *God* for using Pastor Steven Flockhart that day. Pastor Steve walks the walk. He is a man of integrity. May *God* bless Pastor Steve and his family.

Several additional men greatly encouraged me. I want to thank Brad Currie, Ray Hefner, Dana Reed, Johnny Robertson (my Sunday school teacher), and Mike Stewart. The list is endless. I thank *God* again for placing such godly men in my life.

Last and most of all, I would like to thank *God* for the woman who stood behind me for the past 17 years. I owe so much to her. She is my wife, Jean. If I had to repay her for all she has done for me, I would not be able to. She has always been there for me through thick and thin. I thank *God* for her. I know I do not say it enough, but I hope she realizes that she means the world to me and that I love her very much. I am thankful to *God* for saving her also on the same day that I accepted *Jesus* as my personal *Lord* and *Savior.*

In addition, I would like to thank *God* for saving my little girl, Miranda, on May 25, 2005. *God* is so good. *All the time!*

I hope you enjoy the book that *God* has given me the opportunity to write. *God* bless, and have a great day!

Your Brother in *Christ,*
Frank L. Johnson, III

Abducted

So He came to Nazareth, where He had been brought up. And as His custom was, He went into the synagogue on the Sabbath day, and stood up to read. And He was handed the book of the prophet Isaiah. And when He had opened the book, He found the place where it was written:

The Spirit of the Lord is upon Me,
Because He has anointed Me
To preach the gospel to the poor;
He has sent Me to heal the brokenhearted,
To proclaim liberty to the captives
And recovery of sight to the blind,
To set at liberty those who are oppressed;
To proclaim the acceptable year of the Lord.

—Luke 4:16-19

When we arrive in this world through birth, we have no ability to make decisions for ourselves. We are completely dependent upon the person from whom we were born. Therefore, we learn from others by the way they live and act, whether it is good or bad.

At such a young age, we do not know good from bad; we just trust and obey the people around us.

As we grow older, we begin to notice the difference between good and bad. Unfortunately, we often notice that the people around us are doing more bad than good. As we transition from youth into adulthood, we have a feeling there has to be something better out there. We feel like something is holding us back, but we are not sure what that is. It is as if we have been abducted and held captive—and cannot break free of the strongholds.

Who is this abductor? It is Satan. He makes us think we need to pay a ransom, one we cannot afford to pay, to be set free. What we do not realize is the ransom has already been paid in full.

Who could afford to pay such a high price to set us free? God sent His one and only Son, Jesus, who was born, lived among us for thirty-three years, and then died on the cross at Calvary. He paid the price in full. The blood Jesus shed on Calvary was the payment for our freedom from the sins that bind us to this world.

How can you receive this freedom? Simply ask Jesus to come into your life and forgive you of your sins. Jesus will change your life forever and will set you free.

God bless, and have a great day. Go share the good news!

Are You Covered?

This is the message which we have heard from Him and declare to you, that God is light and in Him is no darkness at all. If we say that we have fellowship with Him, and walk in darkness, we lie and do not practice the truth. But if we walk in the light as He is in the light, we have fellowship with one another, and the blood of Jesus Christ His Son cleanses us from all sin.

If we say that we have no sin, we deceive ourselves, and the truth is not in us. If we confess our sins, He is faithful and just to forgive us our sins and to cleanse us from all unrighteousness. If we say that we have not sinned, we make Him a liar, and His word is not in us.

—1 John 1:5-10

You are probably wondering what I mean by, "Are you covered?" Let me tell you. Are you of this world? If you are, sin covers you. You have committed many sins throughout your lifetime on earth. However, you tell yourself, "I haven't sinned that much" or "I'm a pretty good person and my good definitely outweighs my bad."

Unfortunately, one sin is too many, if you have never asked for forgiveness of that one sin. I am not talking about going to another man to confess your sins. I am talking about going to God through His Son, Jesus, and asking Him to forgive you of your sins.

Many people think you cannot go directly to God. They think they need someone who is holy in the eyes of the world to intercede for them. I used to think the same way until Jesus saved me on October 7, 2001, when I repented of my sins and invited Him into my life as my personal Lord and Savior.

There is no man in this world holy enough to go before God on my behalf to ask Him to forgive me of my sins. It is my responsibility to go to God, since it is my sin. This is between God and me. Romans 3:23 tells us, "For all have sinned and fall short of the glory of God."

Unless you know Jesus as your personal Lord and Savior, and have asked Him to save you and forgive you of your sins, you won't have the connection you need to go directly to our heavenly Father. The Bible states, "The only way to the Father is through His Son, Jesus" (John 14:6). It is not through Mary, the mother of Jesus, or any saint. My friend, if you do not believe this, then Jesus' death on the cross for your sins was in vain.

I know and believe that the blood Jesus shed on Calvary was more than enough to cover my sins and yours. All you have to do is surrender your life to Jesus and ask Him to forgive you. It is as easy as **A**, **B**, **C**: **A**dmit you are a sinner; **B**elieve in the death, burial, and resurrection of Jesus Christ, and that He died for you; and **C**onfess your sins with a truly repentant heart.

Let Jesus cover your sin and win! Have a great day!

Back Pains

Come to Me, all *you* who labor and are heavy laden, and I will give you rest. Take My yoke upon you and learn from Me, for I am gentle and lowly in heart, and you will find rest for your souls. For My yoke is easy and My burden is light.

—Matt. 11:28-30

Christians suffer many trials. While we are living in this world, trials and burdens inundate us, which we end up carrying on our backs. Unfortunately, we carry them for so long that we begin to get back pains. We begin to bend under the pressure, which causes us to look down instead of up. Often, we clutch these burdens when we should be releasing them to Jesus.

When Jesus came into the world to save us, He gave us the ability to experience peace and joy in the midst of our trials.

Although He saved us, and we must continue to live in this world, we must not be conformed to this world (Romans 12:2).

Carrying our burdens on our backs throws us off balance in our walk and eventually will cause us to stumble. Sometimes we fall back into our old ways because life seemed so much easier when we conformed to the world. We can mask our pain with something of the world such as drugs, alcohol, food, or sex. This lasts only until we wake up the next morning, however, lying on our backs in an unfamiliar place. That is where we need to be—flat on our backs, not knowing where we are, looking up, and crying out to Jesus.

We always complain when things do not go our way. When we talk about burdens, trials, and back pains, we often forget what Jesus did to get us to where we are today and where He brought us from in our past. Before Jesus, we had a future that ended in death. Now that we have Jesus in our lives, our future leads to everlasting life.

The life we now have with Jesus did not happen without a cost. It cost Jesus His life. Before they crucified Jesus on the cross, He endured great back pain. The soldiers scourged Him with whips and catenae tails, which tore into His back. The Bible says He was beaten beyond recognition (Isaiah 52:14). Imagine the back pain Jesus endured—pain He endured for us because He loved us so much.

If that were not enough, Jesus then had the weight of the world's sin dumped on His shoulders. They weren't only past sins, but also our present and future sins. We complain about the little burdens we have in our lives, when they are nothing compared to what Jesus did for us.

So, stop complaining! Give up your sinful ways and your burdens will be light. Have a great day and keep looking up! God bless!

Backpacking

Now this I say, brethren, that flesh and blood cannot inherit the kingdom of God; nor does corruption inherit incorruption. Behold, I tell you a mystery: We shall not all sleep, but we shall all be changed—in a moment, in the twinkling of an eye, at the last trumpet. For the trumpet will sound, and the dead will be raised incorruptible, and we shall be changed. For this corruptible must put on incorruption, and this mortal *must* put on immortality. So when this corruptible has put on incorruption, and this mortal has put on immortality, then shall be brought to pass the saying that is written: "*Death is swallowed up in victory.*"

"O Death, where is your sting?"
O Hades, where is your victory?"

The sting of death *is* sin, and the strength of sin *is* the law. But thanks *be* to God, who gives us the victory through our Lord Jesus Christ.

> Therefore, my beloved brethren, be steadfast, immovable, always abounding in the work of the Lord, knowing that your labor is not in vain in the Lord.
>
> —1 Cor. 15:50-58

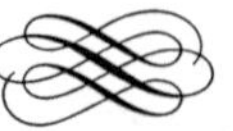

When we go through life without Jesus in our lives, it's as if we are carrying a backpack on our back. The pack starts out light but as we travel through life, the pack takes on a little weight from the sins we committed and held onto. We cinch up the pack a little so we will not feel the weight of our sin as much. Then we begin to feel comfortable with our sin again.

As we continue our sinful walk through life, we may take the wrong path, which leads to more trouble. We always have the ability to turn around. All that sin ends up on our back, stuffed in our backpack. We think we can hide it from the world.

This cycle goes on for years, until our sins become so heavy and we can no longer cinch up our pack. We try one last time but fall flat on our face because the weight of our sin is too much for us to carry. Our sin spills out for the whole world to see. We try to hide our sin by trying to cover it up but we simply cannot. We lie there in the stench of the sin we've hidden for years and wonder how we can get rid of it.

At this point, we realize we are exactly where we need to be—flat on our face, crying out to the only one who can pull us from the pit. That one is Jesus Christ. It was Jesus, who died and shed His blood to cover our sins and free us from bondage.

As we begin our new life in Christ, let us remember to release our sins as quickly as possible so they will not hinder our walk. Remember, we've got the victory! God bless, and have a great day!

Balloons

Have you not known?
Have you not heard?
The everlasting *God*, the LORD,
The Creator of the ends of the earth,
Neither faints nor is weary.
His understanding is unsearchable.
He gives power to the weak,
And to *those who have* no might He increases strength.
Even the youths shall faint and be weary,
And the young men shall utterly fall,
But those who wait on the LORD
Shall renew *their* strength;
They shall mount up with wings like eagles,
They shall run and not be weary,
They shall walk and not faint.

—Isa. 40:28-31

Have you ever looked at your life as if you were a balloon? Balloons are great. They can make people happy when they are sick or sad. They are great at birthday parties, and they can make someone's day a little brighter.

Christians need to live life as if we are a balloon. Life is fragile, just like a balloon. It doesn't take much to change the destiny of either one. All it takes is the wind, a sharp object, or the string holding it back from doing what it does best—flying freely.

Life is the same way. The winds of change can alter our destiny, just as a sharp object can inflict pain and the strings that tie us to our worldly possessions. We need to be more like a balloon. A balloon allows the wind to carry it wherever it takes it. The balloon needs someone to fill it up and someone to relieve its pressure when the heat builds up. It is totally dependent on someone or something to take care of it.

This is like living by faith. We must walk by faith and not by sight (2 Corinthians 5:7). That is why Jesus died on the cross—so we could run to Him whenever we need someone to carry us. He also died so that the Holy Spirit could reside within our hearts and fill us with joy, relieve us of the pressures of the world, cut our ties to the world, and depend on Him and Him alone.

Often, pride, self-sufficiency, and self-preservation fill us up and cause us to become over-inflated. People can see right through you and you are about ready to pop and expose your sin for the world to see.

Before you pop, however, try deflating yourself (die to self) and your sin, and fall flat on your face. Ask God to fill you up with the Holy Spirit and let Him control the pressures and the up and downs in your life. God bless, and have a great day!

Battle Plan Check Point

Finally, my brethren, be strong in the Lord and in the power of His might. Put on the whole armor of God, that you may be able to stand against the wiles of the devil. For we do not wrestle against flesh and blood, but against principalities, against powers, against rulers of the darkness of this age, against spiritual *hosts* of wickedness in the heavenly *places.* Therefore, take up the whole armor of God, that you may be able to withstand in the evil day, and having done all, to stand.
Stand therefore, having girded your waist with truth, having put on the breastplate of righteousness, and having shod your feet with the preparation of the gospel of peace; above all, taking the shield of faith with which you will be able to quench all the fiery darts of the wicked one. And take the helmet of salvation, and the sword of the Spirit, which is the word of God; praying always with all prayer and supplication in the Spirit, being watchful to this end with all perseverance and supplication for all the saints –"

—Eph. 6:10-18

I was driving home the other night, and as I came closer to my hometown, I noticed a bunch of flashing, blue lights. I thought there was an accident or something. I noticed the closer I got, however, that it was a police checkpoint, checking cars and people for drugs and drivers under the influence of alcohol.

Years ago, I would have been scared to death that a police officer would have pulled me over at a checkpoint because I would have been driving under the influence of alcohol. I knew better than to drink and drive, but I didn't think a couple beers would affect me that much. Either way, I was wrong: one drink would have been too many.

I don't drink anymore. A little over three years ago, God graciously took away my desire to drink when He saved me and changed me. I could not have done it without Him.

Christians need to set up a daily checkpoint in our walk with God. We must be accountable in everything we do. Living in this world and being a Christian is hard to do when constantly attacked from every side.

The world is full of so many things that can pull us away from our walk with God. We must prepare ourselves for the battle every day, as stated in Ephesians 6:10-18 (page 25). This letter was from Paul, an apostle of Jesus Christ, who fought the battle every day of his life. That is why Paul said, "Pray for me, too," because he was beaten, thrown in jail more than once, and left to die. However, he never gave up, and he won many battles because he kept his life in check and lived out these verses.

Prepare yourself for battle every day, as Paul did. Every day is a battle. Put on the whole armor of God so you will be prepared to fight, and stand firm. God bless!

Blackboard

If we confess our sins, He is faithful and just to forgive us *our* sins and to cleanse us from all unrighteousness.

—1 John 1:9

Most of us remember back in grade school when we did not listen to the teacher or we were disciplined for something we did wrong. The teacher either sent us to the principal's office or gave us detention. There may have been a time when the teacher made us miss recess or stay after school to write on the blackboard what we did wrong a hundred times. When you got home your mother or father would discipline you again. You couldn't seem to win that day.

Let's look at how we can relate this blackboard to our lives. Before we became Christians, we did a lot of stuff that displeased God. We lived our lives as if there were no tomorrow and sin was no big deal. Nevertheless, if we had to write on the blackboard all the sin we committed and leave it there for the world to see, would it be a big deal then? I think most of us would go into hiding. Hopefully, we would eventually realize we could not hide from our sin because our sin would always find us.

The day we asked Jesus to forgive us of our sins and to come live inside our hearts, He saved us and erased the sins on that blackboard. The teacher (in this case, Jesus Christ) would take the erasers, wipe the board clean, and say, "Your sins have been forgiven. I wiped your sins away. Go now and sin no more."

When Jesus takes the erasers and beats them together, the chalk dust represents our sins. The east and west winds pick up our sins and carry them away, and they are never brought up again.

So, don't get erased by the world. Be wiped clean by the blood of Jesus, which He shed on the cross for your sins. God bless, and have a great day!

Blessings in a Bottle

When He slew them, then they sought Him;
And they returned and sought earnestly for God.
Then they remembered that God *was* their rock,
And the Most High God their Redeemer.
Nevertheless they flattered Him with their mouth,
And they lied to Him with their tongue;
For their heart was not steadfast with Him,
Nor were they faithful in His covenant.
But He, *being* full of compassion, forgave *their* iniquity,
And did not destroy *them*.
Yes, many a time He turned His anger away,
And did not stir up all His wrath;
For He remembered that they *were but* flesh,
A breath that passes away and does not come again.

—Ps. 78:34-39

Have you seen the movie *Aladdin*, the television show *I Dream of Jeannie*, or some type of movie with a genie in it? Often in our Christian walk, we treat God as if He were a genie. If life is going great, money is not a problem, and we have everything we need, we figure we do not need God. We think we can do it on our own.

Essentially, it is as if we are putting God in that genie lamp. We close Him inside, put Him on a shelf, and forget about Him as well as what He did for us through His Son, Jesus. Then we place a sign on the lamp that reads, "Do not open. Only open in case of an emergency."

We might go on like this for years. Then, something happens in our lives: we lose our job, a family member gets sick, or someone dies. The first place we run to is God. We grab the lamp off the shelf and start rubbing it, hoping if we rub it hard and long enough, God will appear from inside the lamp and grant us three wishes. But nothing happens.

What we do not see because of our sinful and ungrateful heart, however, is that God has already granted us three blessings that are better than any wish. He did it through His Son, Jesus, by the death, burial, and resurrection to a new life. It is a life for an eternity.

There isn't any wish out there that can top that or last that long. God bless, and have a great day!

Blood Drive

He is despised and rejected by men,
A Man of sorrows and acquainted with grief.
And we hid, as it were, *our* faces from Him;
He was despised, and we did not esteem Him.
Surely He has borne our griefs
And carried our sorrows;
Yes we esteem Him stricken,
Smitten by God, and afflicted.
But He *was* wounded for our transgressions,
He was bruised for our iniquities;
The chastisement for our peace *was* upon Him,
And by His stripes we are healed.
All we like sheep have gone astray;
We have turned, every one, to his own way;
And the LORD has laid on Him the iniquity of us all.
He was oppressed and He was afflicted,
Yet He opened not His mouth;
He was led as a lamb to the slaughter,

And as a sheep before its shearers is silent,
So He opened not His mouth.
He was taken from prison and from judgment,
And who will declare His generation?
For He was cut off from the land of the living;
For the transgressions of My people He was stricken.
And they made His grave with the wicked –
But with the rich at his death,
Because He had done no violence,
Nor *was any* deceit in His mouth.
Yet it pleased the LORD to bruise Him;
He has put *Him* to grief.
When You make His soul an offering for sin,
He shall see *His* seed, He shall prolong *His* days,
And the pleasure of the LORD shall prosper in His hand.
He shall see the labor of His soul, *and* be satisfied.
By His knowledge My righteous Servant shall justify many,
For He shall bear their iniquities.
Therefore I will divide Him a portion with the great,
And He shall divide the spoil with the strong,
Because He poured out His soul onto death,
And He was numbered with the transgressors,
And He bore the sin of many,
And made intercession for the transgressors.

—Isa. 53:3-12

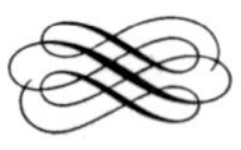

We had a blood drive at work the other day. I donated my usual pint because one never knows who might need a blood transfusion.

After I finished donating, I went through the rest of the day thinking about Jesus and how much blood He sacrificed for you and me on the cross at Calvary. Jesus did not just give a pint of blood and come down off the cross—He gave everything, every drop. He did this to cover the sins of the world, past, present and future. He gave it all out of love for you and me.

I flinched when they pricked my finger to check the iron level in my blood. Then it was time to lie on the padded table to donate blood. They warned me I might feel a little prick, like a bee sting, when they inserted the needle into my arm. Then they stuck me.

Just think of the pain that Jesus went through when they laid Him on that cross. There wasn't any padding on those rough timbers. It was probably full of splinters sticking into His back and into the wounds He received from the beating He endured for your sins and mine. Then they tied ropes around His wrists to stretch His arms, dislocating them from their sockets, which inflicted even more pain—pain we cannot even imagine. Then they grabbed the hammer and nails. I can picture them saying before they drove the nails into His hands and feet, "You might feel a little bee sting," as they mocked Him. I cannot even fathom the pain six-inch nails driven through my hands and feet must feel like. I thank God that Jesus did the will of His Father and went all the way to Calvary to fulfill the purpose He came to earth to do.

The next time there is a blood drive in your hometown, donate a pint in the name of Jesus. God bless, and have a great day!

Bridges

Therefore, since we have such hope, we use great boldness of speech— unlike Moses, *who* put a veil over his face so that the children of Israel could not look steadily at the end of what was passing away. But their minds were blinded. For until this day the same veil remains unlifted in the reading of the Old Testament, because the *veil* is taken away in Christ. But even to this day, when Moses is read, a veil lies on their heart. Nevertheless, when one turns to the Lord, the veil is taken away. Now the Lord is the Spirit; and where the Spirit of the Lord *is*, there *is* liberty. But we all, with unveiled face, beholding as in a mirror the glory of the Lord, are being transformed into the same image from glory to glory, just as by the Spirit of the Lord.

—2 Cor. 3:12-18

What type of bridge are you crossing? Where will the bridge lead you? Is your bridge as secure as your walk, or is your walk as secure as your bridge?

What material you build your bridge on or with determines how secure it will be when you encounter storms in your life. If you built your bridge with wood and cables, like a swinging bridge, it will not be very secure during a storm. It may allow you safe passage, but the fear of crossing it during a storm might sway your decision from side to side, causing you to fall into a pit. Of course, we know there are safer bridges to cross. At least, they appear to be safer. No matter what material we use to build our bridge, it will never withstand all the storms that hit us in our lifetime.

Don't get me wrong—man can build safe-*looking* bridges. Crossing the bridge, however, is not all that matters; where that bridge leads and in what direction it leads after we cross it is equally important.

The most secure bridge for a lost person is a covered bridge. As we cross it, the darkness hides us. Other people cannot see our sins, and as we emerge from the other side, everything seems fine. However, the sin is still in our hearts. If we try to hide our sin by covering it up, eventually it will burden us so much and become like dead weight. The bridge we trusted to hide our sin will not be able to support the weight and will collapse under the strain. Then, the current will wash our sins downstream and expose them to the world.

If you are crossing a bridge in your life, be sure it can carry you safely to the other side. If you build your bridge with things of the world, consider this before you cross: is the bridge strong enough to carry the weight of your trials and sins?

The only bridge I know which is strong enough is the one leading to God! How much does it cost to cross this bridge? Is there a toll? Jesus paid the toll with His life, but your cost is surrendering your life to God. His Son, Jesus, who died on the cross for your sins, provided this bridge to God. The bridge is the cross. It leads to life. You will no longer be separated from God.

Stop crossing bridges that lead nowhere, and cross the bridge that can change your life forever and ever. God bless!

Bungee Cord Christian

Likewise you also, reckon yourselves to be dead indeed to sin, but alive to God in Christ Jesus our Lord.

Therefore do not let sin reign in your mortal body, that you should obey it in its lusts. And do not present your members *as* instruments of unrighteousness to sin, but present yourselves to God as being alive from the dead, and your members as instruments of righteousness to God. For sin shall not have dominion over you, for you are not under law but under grace.

What then? Shall we sin because we are not under the law but under grace? Certainly not! Do you not know that to whom you present yourselves slaves to obey, you are that one's slaves whom you obey, whether of sin *leading* to death, or of obedience *leading* to righteousness? But God be thanked that *though* you were slaves of sin, yet you obeyed from the heart that form of doctrine to which you were delivered. And having been set free from sin, you became slaves of righteousness. I speak in human *terms* because of the weakness of your flesh. For just as you presented your members *as* slaves of uncleanness, and

> of lawlessness *leading* to *more* lawlessness, so now present your members *as* slaves of righteousness for holiness.
>
> —Rom. 6:11-19

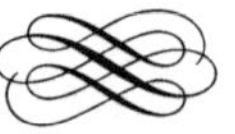

When Jesus saves us, we often treat our salvation like a bungee cord. We do not always release everything from our past to God, as we should. We tend to hold on to those things from our past.

For by grace we have been saved through faith and that not of ourselves; it is the gift of God, not of works, lest anyone should boast (Ephesians 2:8). Unfortunately, many times we treat grace as a bungee cord. We jump back and forth, in and out of our old ways. We use God's grace, which is the recoil from the bungee cord, to pull us away from our sin and back into fellowship with Him. However, the more we abuse this grace, the farther and farther away we find ourselves from God. Every time we jump back into our old ways, there is more and more stress placed on the cord because of all of the weight we have collected from the sin we don't always release. Therefore, every time we jump back into our sin, the deeper into the pit we go. The bungee cord loses its elasticity, and because of all the excess weight and stress applied to the cord, it takes longer to pull us back.

The more time we spend in our sin, the easier it becomes to fall back into the worldly ways. The cord becomes weaker and eventually it snaps in two. Then we fall deep into the pit and become stuck in our sins and the ways of the world. Hopefully, we eventually realize we need to release everything to Jesus if we are ever to have victory and live a life filled with the peace and joy that comes with our salvation.

Release your sin and win! Have a great day! God bless!

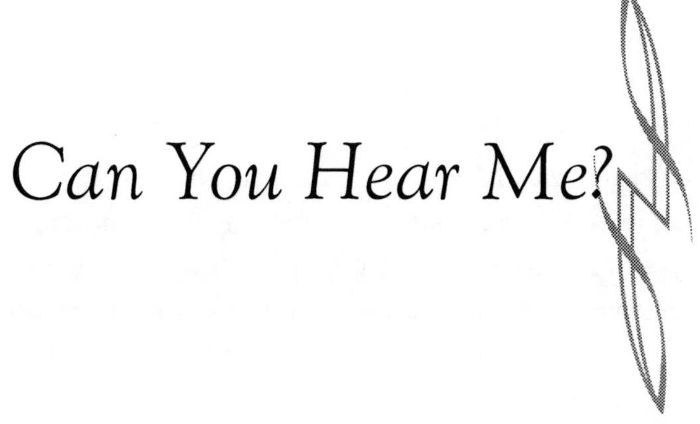

Can You Hear Me?

I will love You, O LORD, my strength.
The LORD is my rock and my fortress and my deliverer;
My God, my strength, in whom I will trust;
My shield and the horn of my salvation, my stronghold.
I will call upon the LORD, *who is worthy* to be praised;
So shall I be saved from my enemies.

—Ps. 18:1-3

Have you ever wondered how good your connection is to God? It all depends on how good your service is to Him. If you have never accepted Jesus as your personal Lord and Savior, your connection is lousy.

The only way to God is through His Son, Jesus Christ (John 14:6), who provided that connection when He died for our sins on the cross at Calvary. Therefore, friend, if you do not have

Jesus and your only connection is to this world, you have a connection from hell—and its service really stinks.

If you would like better service, choose the provider Who will never drop any of your calls. That provider's name is Jesus Christ. He is our strong tower (Proverbs 18:10). When we call on the name of Jesus, every call goes through and He always answers. The connection will remain strong, no matter what type of storm you are going through. It won't matter if you are on a mountaintop, in a valley, or somewhere in between.

Drop your connection to this world before it costs you your life, and receive the connection that can save it. It won't cost you a dime. Jesus paid for the service in full when He died on the cross. All you have to do to receive this service is repent of your sins and surrender your life to Jesus. Do not waste another minute, because no one knows how long this offer will last. It could end at any time. "Don't let your next call be answered with the message: "Sorry this number no longer exists. Please check the number and dial again." The Bible says in 2 Corinthians 6:2, "For He says, '*In an acceptable time I have heard you, And in the day of salvation I have helped you.*' Behold, <u>now</u> is the accepted time; behold, <u>now</u> is the day of salvation." Remember we are not guaranteed another day.

Dial Jeremiah 33:3, which says, "Call to Me, and *I* will answer you, and show you great and mighty things, which you do not know," and never get hung up on again. God bless!

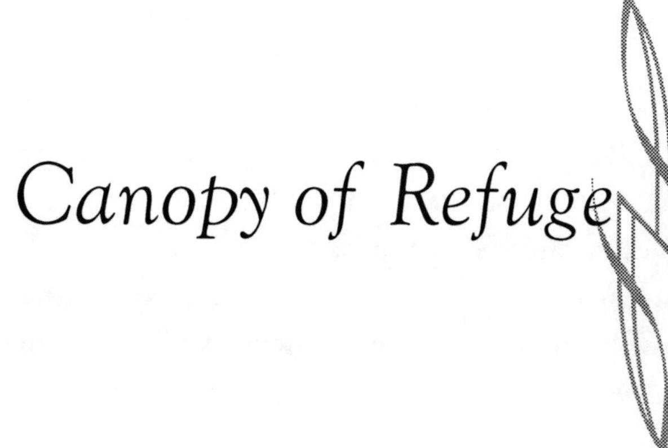

Canopy of Refuge

Whatever my eyes desired I did not keep from them.
I did not withhold my heart from any pleasure,
For my heart rejoiced in all my labor;
And this was my reward from all my labor.
Then I looked on all the works that my hands had done
And on the labor in which I had toiled;
And indeed all was vanity and grasping for the wind.
There was no profit under the sun.

—Eccl. 2:10-11

Have you ever walked from a field into a wooded area and felt the change in temperature? It drops several degrees within seconds because of the protection provided by the canopy of trees.

Most of us spend our lives in the fields, which is the world. That is where we labor away most of our life, trying to make a better life for ourselves. For what—a paycheck? For many of us, a paycheck is just enough money to get us though until the next payday. Every time we think we are getting a little ahead of the game, something happens—perhaps an illness or the arrival of a child—that turns up the heat even more. We spend so much time in the work field that we feel our skin burning from the inside out. It's not sunburn, however; it is a cancer eating away at us. We know we cannot leave the field because we need to provide for our family. Although it is killing us from the inside and we feel the pain, no one else can see it. We try to hide our pain for as long as we can.

Unfortunately, eventually the pain becomes so intense that people around us notice a change. We continue to hit the fields every day, masking the pain with the comforts of the world—drugs, alcohol, food, or some other addiction—which merely prolongs the pain and suffering. We finally collapse in the field. The world keeps working around us as if we don't exist. They step on us, kick us when we are down, and shove us off to the side like useless flesh. That is all we are, anyway, if we rely on the world to sustain us.

Deep within us, however, beneath the flesh and the cancer that's spreading in our bodies, there is a hope—a hope deep within our hearts that God placed there when He created us. A hope we could not see or feel before because we found ourselves trapped inside. The day finally comes when you give up, give in, and cry out to the Lord.

Often, we need to be broken, broken beyond worldly repair but not beyond godly repair. God built a bridge with two boards and three nails. Surely, He can repair your life. All we have to do is surrender our lives to Jesus, the one who stretched out His arms on a cross. His arms form the canopy that will save us and shade us from the world and its heat.

Come to the tree where Jesus died. Fall to your knees, die of your sins today, and receive life from the tree where Jesus died for you. Have a great day, and God bless!

Carpet Fibers

No one puts a piece of unshrunk cloth on an old garment; for the patch pulls away from the garment, and the tear is made worse. Nor do they put new wine into old wineskins, or else the wineskins break, the wine is spilled, and the wineskins are ruined. But they put new wine into new wineskins, and both are preserved."

—Matt. 9:16-17

Many Christian churches do not stand up for what they believe. They are like a carpet, lying there and doing nothing but taking abuse from every angle. They are stepped on, feet are wiped on them, and stuff is dumped on them.

Over time, all this stuff builds up and is ground deep into the fibers. Their once radiant carpets start to fray and the fibers that held them together unravel at the seams from all the stress of sins, such as gossip and disunity. Then they split.

This is what happens to many churches. You hear about it all the time, but it never sinks in until it hits home. Yes, many churches today are on the verge of splitting or closing their doors forever, right in your hometown. People try to repair the torn fibers that have been in the church since the very beginning by bringing in new fibers to repair the old, like putting new wine in old wineskins. These will hold for a while, but once the pain, wounds, and disunity ferment for a while, the pressure becomes so great that the wineskins burst, just like the fibers of the church.

The only way to repair this split is to come together to fast and pray, asking for forgiveness for the unconfessed sin we have been harboring deep in our heart. The Spirit cannot operate in an unclean heart. Let us release everything to Jesus and let Him repair it with His cleansing blood. Only Jesus' blood can give the deep cleansing the church needs.

After cleansing takes place, we can begin to rebuild the church and add new fibers to the carpet, which is the church. Be blessed and not in a mess!

Christian Mathematics 101

Even so the tongue is a little member and boasts of great things.
See how great a forest a little fire kindles! And the tongue *is* a fire, a world of iniquity. The tongue is so set among our members that it defiles the whole body, and sets on fire the course of nature; and it is set on fire by hell. But no man can tame the tongue. *It is* an unruly evil, full of deadly poison. With it we bless our God and Father, and with it we curse men, who have been made in the similitude of God. Out of the same mouth proceed blessing and cursing. My brethren, these things ought not to be so. Does a spring send forth fresh *water* and bitter from the same opening? Can a fig tree, my brethren, bear olives, or a grapevine bear figs? Thus no spring yields both salt water and fresh.

—James 3:5-6, 8-12

Many churches today in America need to take a math test. Most of them are failing in this area, because they do not know how to add or multiply; all they know is how to subtract and divide. God did not intend for us to do that. Jesus went to Calvary to die for our sins so that He could add people to and multiply His kingdom.

Unfortunately, many Christians think about themselves and no one else. They don't serve in the church or share their faith. You may see them at Christmas and Easter, but even the F.B.I. can't find them on Sunday or during the week. It makes you wonder what they are doing with all that free time. Christians need to start multiplying God's kingdom by sharing their faith. There are many who need to hear the good news and all that Jesus did for them on the cross at Calvary.

Then, there are Christians who are always spreading gossip instead of their faith. Talk can ruin the reputation of another person and the church as a whole. Spreading rumors can ruin a person's own testimony. We are all capable of this and don't even know it. We must to stop and think before we speak. We must shut up unless we have something good to say—something that will build up instead of tear down or something that will change a person's life for eternity. Let's step *out* instead of *into* someone else's business unless they ask you for help.

Satan hates math that increases, but God wants us to add and multiply. How do I know this? Well, if you look at the cross, it looks like a big plus sign (which stands for addition). If you tilt the cross, it looks like a multiplication sign. This tells me God wants us to increase His kingdom and not decrease it. The only thing God wants us to subtract from our lives is our sin and pride. He wants to work through and in us for the good of His kingdom.

If you want God to add you to His kingdom, all you have to do is repent of your sins and ask Jesus to come live in your heart and be your Lord and personal Savior. You must mean it with all your heart! Have a great day and God bless!

Classified Ad

For God so loved the world that He gave His only begotten Son, that whoever believes in Him should not perish but have everlasting life. For God did not send His Son into the world to condemn the world, but that the world through Him might be saved.

—John 3:16-17

If God ran a classified ad, how it would read?

> Help wanted. Looking for a person who likes to serve others; who can be tempted but not sin; can be on call 24 hours a day, 7 days a week; can lift lots of dead weight; can nail things down and hang around for a day; can donate blood; can die, be buried, and then rise from the dead in time to be back to work on Monday morning.

Of course, the only one who fits this job description is Jesus Christ. We don't even come close to qualifying for this position.

We might qualify for another classified ad that God might run:

> Looking for a person who cannot find his or her way, who lives in darkness, who is tired of running, and who worships worldly things but is looking for a change.

And the bottom of this classified ad would state:

> Send resume and sin to God the Father, c/o Jesus Christ.

Have a great day, and God bless!

Closets

Have mercy upon me, O God,
According to Your lovingkindness;
According to the multitude of Your tender mercies,
Blot out my transgressions.
Wash me thoroughly from my iniquity,
And cleanse me from my sin.
For I acknowledge my transgressions,
And my sin *is* always before me.
Against You, You only, have I sinned,
And done *this* evil in Your sight–
That You may be found just when You speak,
And blameless when You judge.

—Ps. 51:1-4

What's in your closet? Most people don't know what they have in their closets. It is scary when you think about it;

years upon years of stuff packed away. It's like when you buy a new house with lots of closet space. You have so much room you think you would never be able to fill it up. However, day after day, month after month, and year after year, your closets fill up —much like the sins you fill your life with, hold onto, and never release.

You stash everything in the closet and you try to forget about it. But, every time you open the door to hide more sin, old sin falls off the top shelf—sin you thought was buried and forgotten—spilling onto the floor and opening old wounds.

Eventually, your closets become so full that they burst at the hinges, spilling sin all over your house and into the streets. The sins you have been hiding from family and friends are finally exposed. You try to run and hide, but the weight of your sin finds you out.

Finally, one day you cry out to the only One who can free you from your sin. That one is Jesus Christ. He will take your sins and wash you as white as snow with the blood He shed on the cross at Calvary. He will give you a brand new life.

Let us make a habit of cleaning out our closets on a daily basis to stop the clutter. Have a great day and come out of your closet!

Coffee Cup

The heart knows its own bitterness,
And a stranger does not share its joy.

—Prov. 14:10

If we were to look into your cup of coffee, what would we find? Would your cup be half-full, half-empty, or completely empty?

If you gazed into your cup of coffee, what would you see? If you drink black coffee, you would see a dark reflection. Do you want this reflection to mirror your life? If you like a little cream and sugar in your coffee, it might taste sweet and creamy, but when you look into it, you see a cloudy reflection.

Often, our lives can become clouded like our coffee. Don't get me wrong, I love coffee as much as the next person, but I drink only the regular joe with just a little sugar to take away the bitterness.

Many Christians have unforgiveness and bitterness in their hearts. Have you ever noticed that when someone projects unforgiveness and bitterness, people do not want to be around that person? Resentment and bitterness drip off their lips. Wouldn't it be easy if all we had to do to take away the bitterness was to add a little sugar to our lives? Oh, how great that would be! We can do just that. All we need to do is release our unforgiveness and bitterness to God. He did the sweetest thing anyone could have ever done—He took the darkness in our lives, which is our sin, and had it dumped on His Son, Jesus, at Calvary. Jesus shed His blood and washed away all our sins forever.

The next time you have a cup of java during your quiet time, take a moment to think about what Jesus did for you on the cross. God bless, have a great day, and don't forget to wake up and smell the coffee!

Compass

The LORD will guide you continually,
And satisfy your soul in drought,
And strengthen your bones;
You shall be like a watered garden,
And like a spring of water, whose waters do not fail.
—Isa. 58:11

Have you ever noticed when you look at a map for directions, if you hold it correctly, north is always pointing up? That is how the Christian walk should always be—looking up and walking that straight line.

It sounds easy, but we know that it is not. We do well for a while, and then we stray to the right (east) into sin. Then we stray to the left (west) into even more sin. Sometimes we even fall back, to the south. Often in our walk, when everything seems to be going well, something happens over which we have no control, but we try to solve the problem on our own.

Then it happens. We were sitting idle, and our mind started playing tricks on us. We look east because it is an easier walk, but that does not work. Then we look west because it looks like a way out. When that doesn't work, we fall back south, which stands for our past sins. We get so frustrated that nothing is working out. Then we may fall back into our sinful nature. Suddenly, we find that we traveled so far south; we've ended up flat on our backs, right where we need to be. We should have been looking north, trusting Jesus and not our sinful nature.

Keep your compasses pointing north, toward Jesus, by reading your Bible and praying on a daily basis. He will keep you going in the right direction, north toward Him. God bless, and have a great day!

Convicted or Addicted

Therefore, to him who knows to do good and does not do *it*, to him it is sin.

—James 4:17

When I was born and until I attained salvation at the age of forty, I committed a whole lot of sin. During that time, the sins I committed never bothered me. I did not feel convicted, and at that time, I didn't even know what the word meant in terms of sin. Although raised in church all my life, I had never heard the word "conviction" preached in church. Since I became a Christian, however, I hear and feel the word all the time. Now, if I do anything that is displeasing to God, I feel miserable. Before, if I sinned I would just blow it off, forget about it, and move on. Now that I have Jesus in my life, I cannot simply walk away from my sin.

If Jesus saved you and you hold onto your sin, it will drive you crazy until you ask Him to forgive you. It is hard to walk the Christian walk when you have unconfessed sin in your life. If you proclaim to be a Christian but have no conviction of your sin, you must examine your walk with the Lord. Ask Him to examine your heart and mind. Perhaps you have backslidden.

If your heart does not convict you, then maybe you are addicted to that sin. Being addicted and not convicted can become very dangerous for you and the ones around you. Your addictions can affect you, your marriage, your family, your job, and most of all, your walk with the Lord.

If you have an addiction you cannot let go of, look to the One who can free you. Look to the cross! That is where your help will come from. Psalm 121:2 says, "My help comes from the Lord." All you have to do is believe, live by faith, and let Jesus take control of your heart and your life. Then your convictions can become an addiction—an addiction to follow the One who became addicted to you first, the one who died for your sins—Jesus Christ. Have a blessed day!

Criminal Record

And war broke out in heaven: Michael and his angels fought with the dragon; and the dragon and his angels fought, but they did not prevail, nor was a place found for them in heaven any longer. So the great dragon was cast out, that serpent of old, called the Devil and Satan, who deceives the whole world; he was cast to the earth, and his angels were cast out with him.

Then I heard a loud voice saying in heaven, "Now salvation, and strength, and the kingdom of our God, and the power of His Christ have come, for the accuser of our brethren, who accused them before our God day and night, has been cast down. And they overcame him by the blood of the Lamb and by the word of their testimony, and they did not love their lives to the death. Therefore rejoice, O heavens, and you who dwell in them! Woe to the inhabitants of the earth and the sea! For the devil has come down to you, having great wrath, because he knows that he has a short time."

—Rev. 12:7-12

We are all guilty of a crime (sin). Convicted of this crime, our sentence is death, for the Bible says in Romans 6:23, "for the wages of sin is death, but the gift of God is eternal life in Christ Jesus our Lord."

One day we will face judgment. If you are of this world and follow its ways, you are blind to the truth. You probably will not understand what I am saying. The ruler of this world would like to keep it that way for his benefit. You see, Lucifer was once an angel in heaven. He stood right next to God. However, Lucifer wanted to receive the glory and worship that only God deserves. Therefore, God cast Lucifer out of heaven. The world knows him as Satan or the devil. Satan wants to hide the truth from us because he doesn't want us to receive what he once had. He tries to manipulate us into thinking we have it made. He will take you to your grave believing that unless you repent of your crimes, which are your sins.

You see, Jesus came into this world, but He came out of love because He wanted to. Jesus came to save the world, not to condemn it (John 3:17). He came in the form of a baby, was born of a virgin birth, and lived among His people for thirty-three years. *Jesus* went to Calvary to do His Father's will. There He died on the cross for our sins. He was raised from the dead, ascended into heaven, and is seated at the right hand of His Father.

Satan is here on earth, *not* to save us but to enslave us. Are you willing to keep Satan company, or are you willing to confess your crimes and spend eternity in heaven with Jesus? Jesus will intercede for you and He will set you free through the blood He shed on Calvary. You will one day spend eternity with Jesus in heaven. This is only possible by the grace of God, through faith.

Admit your crimes and let Jesus pardon you with the blood He shed on the Cross! Have a great day, and God bless!

Cross Training

You therefore must endure hardship as a good soldier of Jesus Christ. No one engaged in warfare entangles himself with the affairs of *this* life, that he may please him who enlisted him as a soldier. And also if anyone competes in athletics, he is not crowned unless he competes according to the rules. The hardworking farmer must be first to partake in the crops. Consider what I say, and may the Lord give you understanding in all things.

Remember that Jesus Christ, of the seed of David, was raised from the dead according to my gospel, for which I suffer trouble as an evildoer, *even* to the point of chains; but the word of God is not chained. Therefore I endure all things for the sake of the elect, that they also may obtain the salvation which is in Christ Jesus with eternal glory.

This is a faithful saying:

For if we died with *Him*,
    We shall also live with *Him*.
If we endure,
    We shall also reign with *Him*.
If we deny *Him*,
    He also will deny us.
If we are faithless,
    He remains faithful;
He cannot deny Himself.

—2 Tim. 2:3-13

Cross training is the combination of two exercise regimens. For instance, weight training and aerobics, or swimming and cycling are two good examples. Christians need to do some cross training. We need to begin in the area of serving the Lord in ministry. Just because you serve in one ministry does not mean you cannot serve or cross train in another. The more we do for the Lord by cross training in one or more ministries, the more people we can reach for His Kingdom.

Unfortunately, many of us are not serving even in one ministry. People who do not serve are like spectators in a sporting event. They sit back and watch everyone else around them serve, while they complain about everything that isn't being done. They may have served at one time, but they always have an excuse as to why they can't, won't and don't serve now. The most common excuse I've heard is, "I did my time in the nursery or children's ministry. My kids are all grown up, so why should

I serve in that ministry any more?" and, "I've served my whole life. It's someone else's turn to serve," or, "I don't have the time to serve." You are still alive and kicking, so you haven't served your whole life.

The only one I know who served His whole life is Jesus Christ. He served from the day He was born until the day He died. We know Jesus died on Calvary, but three days later He rose from the dead and ascended into heaven. Although Jesus is in heaven with His Father, He is not as far away as we think He is.

Jesus is still willing to cross train and serve in full capacity if we will only let Him serve from within us and through us. But we need to begin the process; Jesus will not force us to serve. We should be more than willing to serve, however, if we honestly believe in what Jesus went through for us on the cross. "He, that knew no sin, became sin for us" (2 Corinthians 5:21) so we could spend eternity with Him one day in heaven.

If you are not serving, you are probably sinning. What else are you going to be doing with all that extra time you have on your hands? An idle mind is the devil's playground. If you do not serve the Lord, whom are you going to serve? Yourself or Satan? Satan is always taking applications and he will hire you on the spot. If you serve Satan, you will get what you deserve—fired!

Don't let it come to that. Start serving to your full capacity, and the blessings you receive will be more than abundant. Have a great day!

DOA—*Dead on Arrival*

But God, who is rich in mercy, because of His great love with which He loved us, even when we were dead in trespasses, made us alive together with Christ (by grace you have been saved), and raised *us* up together, and made *us* to sit together in the heavenly *places* in Christ Jesus, that in the ages to come He might show the exceeding riches of His grace in *His* kindness toward us in Christ Jesus. For by grace you have been saved through faith, and that not of yourselves; *it is* the gift of God, not of works, lest anyone should boast. For we are His workmanship, created in Christ Jesus for good works, which God prepared beforehand that we should walk in them.

—Eph. 2:4-10

Much of the world is dying and going to hell, and the sad thing is they do not even know it. Many have the notion that if their good outweighs their bad, they will go to heaven when they die. What they don't realize is that one can never be good enough to get into heaven. In addition, they will find no weights and measures in heaven, measuring their good against their bad.

Another misconception the world has about heaven is that you can work your way into it. Many think the more works you do, the better off you will be in heaven and the better position you will hold. No matter how many works you do, they are nothing more than filthy rags (Isaiah 64:6). Those who believe the concept about being good enough or doing good works to get to heaven are in for a shock when they stand before God and the great white throne of judgment. They will find themselves cast into the lake of fire, instead of spending eternity in heaven. They will be dead on arrival and don't even know it. Acts 16:31 says, "Believe on the Lord Jesus Christ, and you will be saved."

So, let us tell everyone about the way Jesus provided for us to get to heaven—by His death, burial, and resurrection to life—and have them arrive alive!

Dandelions

"I am the true vine, and My Father is the vinedresser. Every branch in Me that does not bear fruit He takes away; and every *branch* that bears fruit He prunes, that it may bear more fruit. You are already clean because of the word which I have spoken to you. Abide in Me, and I in you. As the branch cannot bear fruit of itself, unless it abides in the vine, neither can you, unless you abide in Me.

I am the vine, you are the branches. He who abides in Me, and I in him, bears much fruit; for without Me you can do nothing. If anyone does not abide in Me, he is cast out as a branch and is withered; and they gather them and throw *them* into the fire, and they are burned. If you abide in Me, and My words abide in you, you will ask what you desire, and it shall be done for you. By this My Father is glorified, that you bear much fruit; so you will be My disciples.

—John 15:1-8

Dandelions are one of the most common weeds and one of the most difficult to get rid of. You can pull them up, but if you do not get the whole root out, the dandelion will grow back in a couple of days, and several more will come up with it. The dandelion has a taproot that can be up to two feet long (and sometimes longer), so you rarely get the whole root when you pull them up. The dandelion also has a flower that starts out yellow, and after about a week, the flower dries up and turns white. The bloom you see contains hundreds of seeds. They spread like wildfire, either by the wind or from a child blowing on the flower and spreading the seeds everywhere.

Christians can learn a lot from the dandelion. You see, the dandelion has a root that sets itself deep into the ground, giving it strength and stability, and no matter how often we pull on it, step on it, or cut down, it comes back—often stronger than before. If we, however, went through all that pulling, trampling, or cutting, most of us wouldn't get back up. We would probably give up.

Another thing we can learn from the dandelion is how to spread the good news of Jesus Christ. The dandelion spreads its seeds by faith. It depends totally on the wind to survive. Often, our faith is so little that we cannot accomplish anything. On the other hand, although the dandelion's lifespan might last only two weeks, in that period of time it spreads more seeds than we will probably spread in our lifetime. Let us set our roots deep in the Word of God and spread the seeds of life throughout our neighborhoods, workplace, and cities.

The dandelion is a lot like Jesus. In the same way that many people hate dandelions, many people hated Jesus. People want to kill dandelions in the same way people wanted to kill Jesus.

They thought they had won when the dandelions died but the dandelions rose again, just as Jesus rose from the dead three days later.

Do not be a common weed! Be a weed willing to die in order to spread seeds in the fertile fields God has prepared for us.

Decontamination

Behold, I was brought forth in iniquity,
And in sin my mother conceived me.
Behold, You desire truth in the inward parts,
And in the hidden *part* You will make me to know wisdom.
Create in me a clean heart, O God,
And renew a steadfast spirit within me.
Do not cast me away from Your presence,
And do not take Your Holy Spirit from me.
—Ps. 51:5-6, 10-11

We are born into a sinful world with no choice in the matter. As we grow older and have the ability to make decisions for ourselves, however, the decisions we make are often wrong. This can become very dangerous, depending on who or what we hang around. The more wrong decisions we make, the more contaminated we become.

You may be wondering what I am taking about. Well, the more you sin, the more contaminated you become. The more contaminated you become, the more impure you are. Suddenly, something begins to stink. You try to find out where the smell is coming from and realize it is your own stench. You begin to hide because you do not want anyone else to smell the odor of your sin. Finally, it reaches the point to where you cannot stand it. You try to clean yourself up, but it is no use. Sometimes the stench disappears for a couple days, but then it returns, so you go back into hiding again, back into the darkness.

Finally, you realize you cannot handle this by yourself, so you search for help but cannot find it anywhere in this world because you are looking in all the wrong places. The world, which is Satan's stomping ground, doesn't want you to find help, because if you do, he will lose you. Satan would no longer be able to control you and he would hate that.

Where do you find the help you need? In Jesus! Jesus is the One who died for your sins, past, present, and future. The blood He shed on Calvary is the decontaminator you need to cleanse yourself from all your sins. All you have to do is surrender your life to Him and repent of your sins. It is a gift that won't cost you anything. However, it cost Jesus everything.

Let us get cleaned up and live for Jesus. God bless, and have a great day!

Directory

But I saw no temple in it, for the Lord God Almighty and the Lamb are its temple. The city had no need of the sun or of the moon to shine in it, for the glory of God illuminated it. The Lamb *is* its light. And the nations of those who are saved shall walk in its light, and the kings of the earth bring their glory and honor into it. Its gates shall not be shut at all by day (there shall be no night there). And they shall bring the glory and the honor of the nations into it. But there shall by no means enter in anything that defiles, or causes an abomination or a lie, but only those who are written in the Lamb's Book of Life.

—Rev. 21:22-27

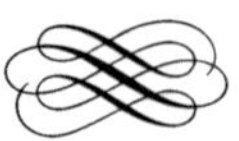

When we walk into an office building, the first thing we look for is the directory to find out where we need to go. When we get to heaven, we will look for a similar directory.

The directory in this case would be the *Lamb's Book of Life*. We will look at this list for our name. There will be many names in this book, and many names will not be there. As we look up and down the list, some of us will find our names quickly and enter heaven. Others will search for days for their name but will never find it. By the time these people finally get to the end of the list, they will be very discouraged and dismayed. They will wonder why their name is not on it. They will think, "My good definitely outweighed my bad." Then they will look around to discover there are no scales to weigh their good works.

When they refer again to the *Lamb's Book of Life*, they will notice the fine print at the bottom of the last page: "For God so loved the world that He gave His only begotten Son, that whoever believes in Him should not perish but have everlasting life" (John 3:16). Imagine that it could go on to read, "Below this verse, if your name does not appear in this book, follow the signs to the courthouse to plead your case." As they follow the signs to the courthouse, they will notice a sudden change in temperature, from cool to hot. Then they will see a huge, white throne. As they begin to hear crying and wailing, they will turn and run. However, they will find that the road behind them has disappeared! They will feel a force pushing them toward the judgment throne. Then, all of a sudden, they will wake up in a cold sweat, scared to death and trembling.

Stop dreaming about waking up in hell! Repent of your sins and ask Jesus to come into your life to be your personal Lord and Savior. Let Him change you and make you a new person. You will then find your name written in the *Lamb's Book of Life*. Make heaven a reality. Have a great day and God bless!

Disobedient Dogs

Let us therefore be diligent to enter that rest, lest anyone fall according to the same example of disobedience. For the word of God *is* living and powerful, and sharper than any two-edged sword, piercing even to the division of soul and spirit, and of joints and marrow, and is a discerner of the thoughts and intents of the heart. And there is no creature hidden from His sight, but all things *are* naked and open to the eyes of Him to whom we *must give* account.

—Heb. 4:11-13

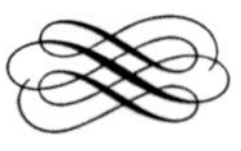

Imagine if we would compare Christians to dogs because sometimes we act just like them. If you think about it, we are often disobedient to our Master. We don't come when called, and we often bite the hand that feeds us. When our Master tells us to sit and stay, we do just the opposite and run away. When

Jesus saved us, He essentially rescued us from the dog pound (sin and death).

Why, then, doesn't our Master just chain us or fence us in? He knows that some of us will either jump the fence or dig a hole under the fence to get out again. Either our own chain or the dogcatcher, which is the world we live in, catches us. Then we find ourselves back where we started from—back in the pound and back in our sin. Our Master sees that our disobedience has gotten us into trouble. Despite that, He again bails us out with His grace, as long as we come to Him with a truly repentant heart, because He loves us so much. We should do the same. We need to return the love our Master shows us through our obedience toward Him. We, however, must remember, there are consequences for our actions and lack of obedience.

Unfortunately, we get so busy with our lives that we forget we once were lost in a world that kept us on a leash, just like a dog. The world has a choker collar around our neck that leads us wherever it wants us to go. This leash can be anything we allow to control our lives, such as money, possessions, alcohol, drugs, sex—or anything that pulls us away from God.

We must stop hiding our sins in the holes we dig. As a dog buries his bone, we bury our sin and then act as if we are the only one who knows where we buried it. Unfortunately, with so many dogs in the world, your sin will be dug up and either exposed to the world or eaten by it.

It is a dog-eat-dog world out there. Let us stop begging like a dog for a bone, become more obedient as we should be, fall to our knees, put our tail between our legs, and ask God for forgiveness. It is by the grace of God we are saved. We need to be more obedient, as Jesus was. He showed His obedience to

His Father by going all the way to Calvary to die for our sins. We need show our obedience by staying in the Word and not in the world. We must stop digging holes and burying our sins. Instead, let us dig up our sin and give them to God. God bless, and have a great day!

Doors

"Behold, *I* stand at the door and knock. If anyone hears My voice and opens the door, *I* will come in to him and dine with him, and he with Me."

—Rev. 3:20

Most of us have a door in our lives. It could be a swinging door or maybe a revolving door. It could be a sliding door or maybe even a screen door. Let us look at these different types of doors.

A swinging door is for people who cannot make up their minds. They are always coming in and out of their door. Every time their door swings open, something comes into their lives. It's like summertime, when every time you open your door a fly gets into the house. The fly you let in can be compared to the sin you let in your life every time you swing your door open.

However, that one sin you let in will multiply once it comes into your life. It starts laying its eggs of deceit.

The next door is a revolving door. This type of door isn't any better than the last door we looked at. It never closes. It is constantly spinning around. It acts like a pump, which pulls in sin from the outside world. It is a hard door to control, because once you let one sin in, other sins are sure to follow. Because sin is constantly pushing your door around, it is always spinning.

The next type of door is a sliding door. It is a little better than the first two doors, but not much. The sliding door is usually made of two big panes of glass. You can see right through them—which is fine, as long as you are not trying to hide anything. However, we are often trying to hide something, so we draw the curtains. The biggest problem is we have control over this type of door. Often, when we are in control, things get out of hand. It is so easy to slide into sin but it is not as easy to slide back out of the sin.

The last type of door is the screen door. It is the worst type of door. When it is closed, sin is still able to penetrate your life. When I consider the screened door, I think of it as protection, because things that fly into it hit the screen. Nevertheless, if you look at it in a negative way, sometimes the smallest particles (sins) can penetrate it. It has some protection but not enough. So, the screen door always exposes you to the sin of the world, because nothing can stop the sin of the world from creeping into your life.

Not one of these doors mentioned can protect us from the sin that infiltrates our lives on a daily basis. However, we have forgotten about one door. It is a strong door. Let us call it the storm door. This door covers the first door in your life and protects it from anything that comes against it.

Where can I find it? You can find this door in the Lord Jesus, who is the door that will protect you through the storms that come against you in your life. Where can I buy this door? You cannot buy it, but you can receive it. All you have to do is open your first door, cry out to Jesus, and ask Him to forgive you of your sins, come into your life, and change you. Allow Him to cover you with His blood, which is the storm door that will protect you and keep you from the sin of the world.

After Jesus installs your storm door and you hear a knock on your door, don't answer it. Let Jesus answer it, because He can handle anything that comes your way. So keep your doors closed and your heart open to the Lord Jesus Christ. Have a great day, and lock your doors to the world!

Elevator

I waited patiently for the LORD;
And He inclined to me,
And heard my cry.
He also brought me up out of a horrible pit,
Out of the miry clay,
And set my feet upon a rock,
And established my steps.
He has put a new song in my mouth—
Praise to our God;
Many will see *it* and fear,
And will trust in the LORD.

—Ps. 40:1-3

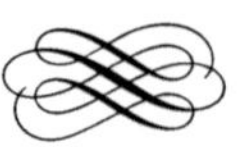

Our Christian walk has many ups and downs, kind of like an elevator. Before Jesus saved us, our lives seemed meaningless. We were in a pit, just like one at the bottom of an elevator shaft. We were at the lowest point in our lives, constantly hammered by the world, which is the elevator. Every time the elevator comes down, it knocks us back into our pit.

Sometimes, it seems we will never make it out of the pit. It is true. We can never get out under our own strength. We need to surrender our lives to Jesus. He is the only one who can pull us from our pitiful life and place us inside the elevator, instead of under it. Just because we are now inside, however, does not mean we should forget from where Jesus pulled us. If we stop trusting in Jesus to guide us through life's ups and downs, we may find ourselves back in the pit.

So, as we move through different levels of our walk and the elevator stops, the doors open, don't get off unless you feel led by the Holy Spirit. If we step off because of our sinful nature or something we see, watch out! When the doors reopen, the elevator might not be there and where do we end up? Back in the pit! So watch your step and keep trusting in Jesus!

Emergency Lighting

He who believes in Him is not condemned; but he who does not believe is condemned already, because he has not believed in the name of the only begotten Son of God. And this is the condemnation, that the light has come into the world, and men loved darkness rather than light, because their deeds were evil. For everyone practicing evil hates the light and does not come to the light, lest his deeds should be exposed. But he who does the truth comes to the light, that his deeds may be clearly seen, that they have been done in God.

—John 3:18-21

Jesus came into this darkened world to bring us the light and the hope of salvation. Because we are sinners and live in the darkness, however, we tend to shy away from the light. Because the light exposes our sin—the sin we have become so comfortable with that we don't even notice anymore. However, if we would simply run to the light, we would see just how much sin we really have in our lives and realize we need the light that we find in Jesus Christ.

Jesus is our emergency light when we lose our ability to see. We find ourselves stumbling in the darkness. Jesus Christ is the light of the world (John 8:12). He will guide us out of the darkness and our sin and back into the light to bring us into fellowship with Him. So, if you are of this world and don't know Jesus as your Lord and personal Savior, you are in the dark.

The world will continue to keep you in the dark as long as you allow it. Run as fast as you can toward the light before the world leads you so far into the darkness that you won't know which way is out. It will all look the same in dark—endless and hopeless. So switch from the darkness to the light and never be the same again.

Run to Jesus! He is your only hope. God bless, and have a great day!

Erosion

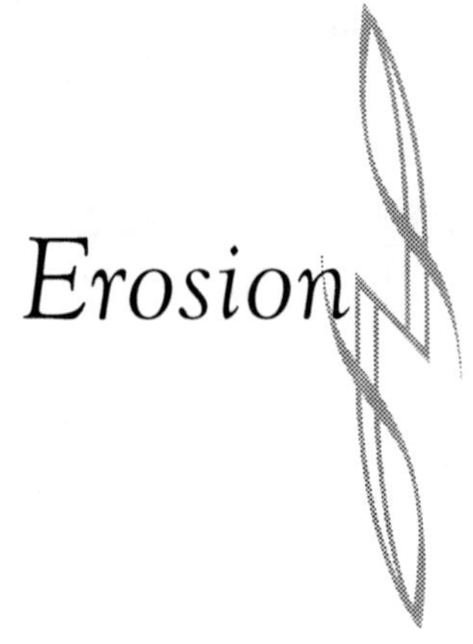

"For as the rain comes down, and the snow from heaven,
And do not return there,
But water the earth,
And make it bring forth and bud,
That it may give seed to the sower
And bread to the eater,
So shall My word be that goes forth from My mouth;
It shall not return to Me void,
But it shall accomplish what I please,
And it shall prosper *in the thing* for which I sent it.
For you shall go out with joy,
And be led out with peace;
The mountains and the hills
Shall break forth into singing before you,
And all the trees of the field shall clap *their* hands.
Instead of the thorn shall come up the cypress tree,
And instead of the brier shall come up the myrtle tree;
And it shall be to the Lord for a name,
For an everlasting sign *that* shall not be cut off."

—Isa. 55:10-13

Let us look at our lives as if we are a river and the world is the bank that surrounds our water. Generally, the two get along great. They work together like a team. We, the river, supply the water to keep the banks green with grass and trees. In turn, the trees shade our waters, keeping us cool, and the grass holds back mud and dirt, which is the sin that can pollute our waters.

But let something come in between the two—a storm, a conflict, or a drought—and watch what takes place. Things begin to change. The banks we once trusted begin allowing dirt to infiltrate our waters. The shade it once provided is gone. Then we have a drought. The waters dry up and the banks that once relied on us for water lose their nourishment. They are no longer lush and green. The grass turns brown, dries up, and withers away, leaving the banks unprotected. They become a battleground between the world and us. When a storm comes our way, the water begins to rise again. With rising waters and the pounding rain, the unprotected banks erode and the dirt, which is sin, washes away from the banks.

After the storm, we, the river, feel violated. So much dirt has washed into our waters that it diminished the flow we once had. Our waters become stagnant from all the sin that has washed into us. The smell from our sin fills the air. Life in our waters has almost ceased to exist. Our river is slowly dying because the sin has choked our flow and holds it back like a dam.

We cannot do anything about it in our own strength. We need the cleansing flood we find in Jesus Christ. We need to repent of our sins and trust and believe in Jesus, let Him handle the flow in our life, and let Him—not the world—hold us within our boundaries. Have a great day!

Escape or Delete

Has then what is good become death to me? Certainly not! But sin, that it might appear sin, was producing death in me through what is good, so that sin through the commandment might become exceedingly sinful. For we know that the law is spiritual, but I am carnal, sold under sin. For what I am doing, I do not understand. For what I will to do, that I do not practice; but what I hate, that I do. If, then, I do what I will not to do, I agree with the law that *it is* good. But now, *it is* no longer I who do it, but sin that dwells in me. For I know that in me (that is, in my flesh) nothing good dwells; for to will is present with me, but *how* to perform what is good I do not find. For the good that I will *to do*, I do not do; but the evil I will not *to do*, that I practice. Now if I do what I will not *to do*, it is no longer I who do it, but sin that dwells in me.

I find then a law, that evil is present with me, the one who wills to do good. For I delight in the law of God according to the inward man. But I see another law in my members, warring

> against the law of my mind and bringing me into captivity to the law of sin which is in my members. O wretched man that I am! Who will deliver me from this body of death? I thank God—through Jesus Christ our Lord!
> So then, with the mind I myself serve the law of God, but with the flesh the law of sin.
>
> —Rom. 7:13-25

Wouldn't it be nice if we had a button we could press to get us out of our sin? We would call this button an Escape button. We could press it and leave our sin. Just because we would escape from our sin, however, does not mean God forgave us of that sin. We are sinners just the same.

Perhaps we could have another button that could erase our sin. We would call this one the Delete button. We could press this button, and our sins would be gone. We could try to edit our sins by changing or correcting them to make them sound not so bad.

This all sounds promising, but there is no way it is possible. We cannot delete, escape, or edit our sins or anybody else's. Romans 3:23 says, "For all have sinned and fall short of the glory of God."

Unfortunately, many religions think a man can listen to your sins and then go to God on your behalf and ask Him to forgive you. It is your sin and it is between you and God. Being a sinner, there is no way you can talk to God on your own.

How and who will free me from my sins, if I cannot talk to God and ask for forgiveness? Well, that is where Jesus comes in. You see, God sent His Son, Jesus, into the world to save us. His death freed us. The blood Jesus shed on the cross is what will delete our sins and open up the communication gap between God and us. We need to repent of our sins and ask Jesus to come live in our hearts and change us forever.

Escape your sin and delete yourself from the world, and let Jesus edify your life. Have a great day, and God bless!

Final Destination

> But you be watchful in all things, endure afflictions, do the work of an evangelist, fulfill your ministry.
>
> —2 Tim. 4:5

Have you ever sat in an airport, watching people rushing around trying to catch their next flight? It is interesting to watch the things they try to accomplish between one gate and the next. It's like watching a marathon take place: people making phone calls, grabbing a bite to eat, running to the bathroom, and then sprinting to their gate to catch their flight.

I will never forget the last time my family and I flew on a plane. We missed our flight. We had to wait five hours to catch the next flight. Now that I think about it, it was in God's plan that we missed our flight. It was for a reason, but I didn't realize until it was too late. Once we arrived home, however, I realized that we had missed a great opportunity. God placed us in that terminal to be a witness for Him, but we failed Him in a big way.

One definition for the word "terminal" results in death. We saw hundreds of people in the terminal to whom we could have witnessed, but we were so upset about missing our flight that all we thought about was our own situation. We didn't stop to think about anyone else's final destination. We didn't think about where they were going to spend eternity—whether they would be going to heaven or hell.

As soon as you walk into an airport, what is the first thing you look at? Everyone looks at the departure and arrival times. If you are a Christian, that schedule should stop you and make you think of those who will be departing from this world and arriving in hell and not even knowing it.

Next time you are in any type of terminal, whether it is a train, bus, or airport terminal, look at all the people around you. Think about how you could change their destination from "terminal" to "eternal." God bless, and have a great day!

Fishing for Sin or Men

Blessed is the man who endures temptation; for when he has been approved, he will receive the crown of life which the Lord has promised to those who love Him. Let no one say when he is tempted, "I am tempted by God"; for God cannot be tempted by evil, nor does He Himself tempt anyone. But each one is tempted when he is drawn away by his own desires and enticed. Then, when desire has conceived, it gives birth to sin; and sin, when it is full-grown, brings forth death.

—James 1:12-15

In many ways, we can compare life to fishing. "How is that," you ask. Well, if you live in the same world I live in, something or someone has probably tempted you at some time or another. The world is a hard place for a Christian to live. Every day is full of trials and temptations aimed toward us, to see what we are made of and if we are what we really say we are.

Picture temptation as the line, sin is the boat, and the world as a body of water in which we live. We are the fish. The boat, which is sin, has many things it can cast out at us, things that look pleasing to the eye, things that catch our attention, and things that can become dangerous if we choose to venture there. The more things the world casts in our path, however, the more comfortable we will become with them, and soon they will no longer look as dangerous to us. We find ourselves taking a little nibble, and then another nibble, and suddenly we want the whole thing. Then we are hooked. The world has you right where it wants you—hook, line, and sinker. It wants to control you.

You try to run, but the line gets tighter and the hook sinks deeper into your flesh, inflicting more pain. It reminds you of the sins you have gotten yourself in. You hide in the shadows of the deep, trying to cover your sin, but as long as you are attached to the world and nibbling at temptation, which is the line, it will keep pulling you out of the shadows to expose your sin again and again.

The world will never release you. It does not practice the catch-and-release program. It practices the catch-and-defeat program. If the world does anything, it will drag you into more sin.

How I can free myself from sin? You cannot do it by yourself. You need someone who stood the test of time, the One who led a sinless life, even when tempted by the world and Satan. His name is Jesus Christ. Jesus can cut the line, which is your temptation, unhook you from the world, take you out of the boat, which is sin, and set you free. He will set you back gently into the water, which is the world.

Although we are to continue living in this world until He returns to bring us home, we are not to be conformed to the world. Jesus tackled death, hell, and the grave, and He did it out of love for you and for me. Jesus has the best tackle out there. You see, His Father handed it down to Him as a gift. God tells us we should be fishers of men, and He has given us the same tackle He gave His Son, Jesus. We just need to read it and believe it, so we will know how to use it when we need it. I am talking about the Word of God, which is the Bible. It can tackle anything that comes your way. God bless, and have a great day!

Focus

When my heart is overwhelmed;
Lead me to the rock that is higher than I.

—Ps. 61:2

Have you ever looked through the lens of a camera and tried to focus in on an object that caught your attention? Perhaps you couldn't get the angle or shot you wanted, or the object got up and left before you were able to take the picture.

Our lives are kind of the same way. Often, we focus our attention on many things at one time. Then we never complete any of the things we set out to accomplish; we become so overwhelmed with everything we are trying to achieve that we get nothing finished. We need to slow down and focus on one thing, complete that task, and then move to the next thing.

Our Christian walk is kind of the same way. We focus on things of the world when we should be focusing on the things of God. Because God never takes His focus off us, we try to run out of the picture. However, God sees the big picture. We cannot hide from God's camera lens. It has a 360-degree view of our life and our sins.

Therefore, run all you want. You will be running in circles and eventually it will lead you back to God. Therefore, stop and get focused on one thing—God. If you start developing your walk with God, you will stop being so negative toward the things God has planned for you.

Let God take all the negatives out of your life and let Him develop them into positive pictures of your future life with Him. God bless! Smile, and don't be camera shy!

For Sale by Owner

> Then Jesus said to His disciples, "If anyone desires to come after Me, let him deny himself, and take up his cross, and follow Me. For whoever desires to save his life will lose it, but whoever loses his life for My sake will find it. For what profit is it to a man if he gains the whole world, and loses his soul? Or what will a man give in exchange for his soul? For the Son of Man will come in the glory of His Father with His angels, and then He will reward each according to his works."
>
> —Matt. 16:24-27

Most people go through life selling themselves as if they were pieces of property. Most often, they sell themselves to the highest bidder. I did this for so many years, trying to find the highest paying job in my line of work—no matter what the consequences were, and regardless of the effect it had on my family or me.

We are always chasing the almighty dollar while trying to get ahead when, in actuality, we are falling behind. We are running out of time. We can never replace time with any amount of money. That is Satan's number one job, to try to destroy our families, our church family, and us.

Let us take the sign off our life that reads, "For Sale by Owner," and replace it with a sign that reads, "Sold Out for Jesus. No More Offers Accepted." Satan would hate to see this happen. He would rather see signs such as, "Contract Pending," "Foreclosure," or "Bankrupt." Sometimes it takes one of these signs to make us realize we need more in life than just money. What we need is Jesus Christ. He is the one who bought us with His blood. It's a done deal. Jesus signed, sealed, and delivered us by His blood.

Stop trying to sell yourself. Give it all to Jesus. He has paid the price in full. God bless, and have a great day!

Free Delivery

I sought the LORD, and He heard me,
And delivered me from all my fears.
The righteous cry out, and the LORD hears,
And delivers them out of all their troubles.
The LORD is near to those who have a broken heart,
And saves such as have a contrite spirit.
Many *are* the afflictions of the righteous,
But the LORD delivers him out of them all.

—Ps. 34:4, 17-19

Have you ever wondered where the term "free delivery" came from? Everyone knows it came from the restaurant business. At one time, it drew in more customers by making it convenient for them to order a meal and have it delivered to their homes or places of business in thirty minutes or less.

Ever since I became a Christian, I have looked at "free delivery" in a different way. When Jesus saved me in October of 2001, He came into my life and forgave me of all my past sins. Jesus delivered me from my sins and my shame, and it didn't cost me anything. It's the best free delivery I have ever received, and it took less than thirty minutes. I didn't even have to give Him a tip. Instead, Jesus gave me a tip: Jesus wants us to go and tell the world of the goodness we received from Him and not to cease spreading the good news until His return.

So, if you are looking for a good delivery service, look to the cross. It's where Jesus delivered us from death, hell, and the grave. He can deliver you, also. All you have to do is call out to Jesus. He is always on time. Ask Him to deliver you from your sins and shame, and you will never again have your sin take you to lunch. Let God bless you, and have a great day!

Garbage

The LORD also will be a refuge for the oppressed,
A refuge in times of trouble.
And those who know Your name will put their trust in You;
For You, LORD, have not forsaken those who seek You.
—Ps. 9:9-10

When Jesus saves us and we give our lives to Him, we are supposed to give all our sins and garbage to Him so that He can take it away from us. However, we always want to hold onto something from the past that we liked to do. It's as if we still have a garbage can in our lives, but we must empty it before we can start to grow in our Christian walk. There is stuff in the trash can we wouldn't want anybody to see, and which we wouldn't trust anybody with—not even the One who died to take it all away. We also must die to self and our past sins, but we don't want to surrender them fully to the Lord Jesus. It's as if we have a recycle bin in our lives like the one on our computer. We dump stuff that we want to get rid of but cannot quite let go of yet.

The things we save in our recycle bins are the very things that cause us to sin and fall short in our walk with God. We must allow God to have access to our recycle bins and let Him empty everything in them: if we went in there, we probably wouldn't empty them. We would continue to fill them to where they overflowed. Satan is always reminding us of our past, so why should we make his job easier by reminding ourselves of our rubbish?

Give your past to God, and let Him recycle your soul and keep you out of the junk pile. God bless, and have a great day!

Getting to the Core

And He said to them, "Do you not understand this parable? How then will you understand all the parables? The sower sows the word. And these are the ones by the wayside where the word is sown. When they hear, Satan comes immediately and takes away the word that was sown in their hearts. These likewise are the ones sown on stony ground who, when they hear the word, immediately receive it with gladness; and they have no root in themselves, and so endure only for a time. Afterward, when tribulation or persecution arises for the word's sake, immediately they stumble. Now these are the ones sown among thorns; *they are* the ones who hear the word, and the cares of this world, the deceitfulness of riches, and the desires for other things entering in choke the word, and it becomes unfruitful. But these are the ones sown on good ground, those who hear the word, accept *it*, and bear fruit: some thirty-fold, some sixty and some a hundred."

—Mark 4:13-20

The church is like an apple. Every time a rumor starts, it's like taking a bite out of your church, which is the apple. Even as I am writing this, there are so many rumors flying around our church that the apple is almost to the core. Most people would see this as the end, and throw it away and say it's over. However, a true Christian would see it as a new beginning.

You can take the core of the church, which is the apple, take the seeds from its core, and re-sow them. Some will be trampled under foot as it falls to the ground, the birds will eat some, and some will fall on rocky soil and die, but the ones that fall on fertile soil will flourish.

Remember, you will always have a few bad apples, but the good apples will always outweigh the bad. So let us pray for unity in our church and for the rumors to end.

Guard Rails

> Therefore, having been justified by faith, we have peace with God through our Lord Jesus Christ, through whom also we have access by faith into this grace in which we stand, and rejoice in hope of the glory of God. And not only *that*, but we also glory in tribulations, knowing that tribulation produces perseverance; and perseverance, character; and character, hope. Now hope does not disappoint, because the love of God has been poured out in our hearts by the Holy Spirit who was given to us.
>
> —Rom. 5:1-5

Christians have a tough road to travel—one full of trials, temptations, and persecution. We need all the help we can get. We can receive that help through the Lord Jesus who is always with us. The road we walk has one lane in each direction. One lane heads in the right direction and the other leads in the wrong direction. What I mean is that once you receive Jesus as your Lord and personal Savior, you want to move in the right direction, heading straight and only looking forward. You do not want to look back.

You notice, however, there are always more people heading the wrong way, the opposite from which you are heading, and you wonder why. These people are still of the world and, unfortunately, most of them do not know any better. They do not want to give up their sin because they are having too much fun.

That is where Christians come in. We have to be very careful of how we approach these people, however, because they may pick us up, knock us down, and drag us down the wrong path. We have been there already and should not want or need to return to our old sin. We have to keep our guardrails in place, because if we let them down, we ask for trouble. Once we let our guard down, we set ourselves up for a fall. This could also tempt us to fall back into our old ways and cause us to get off course; otherwise, we will have to start all over again. It is a long road back to where you were before you fell.

So, keep your guardrails up, be a witness, and keep heading in the right direction. Eventually, the others will notice, and once they do, they become curious and start asking you questions. That is when you surround them with your guardrails, show them the love of Jesus, and tell them they are heading in the wrong way. Draw others to you by your witness.

Keep your eyes focused on your future and not your past, keep your guardrails in place, and never let them down. Have a great day and God bless!

Guide Dog

If you instruct the brethren in these things, you will be a good minister of Jesus Christ, nourished in the words of faith and of the good doctrine which you have carefully followed. But reject profane and old wives' fables, and exercise yourself toward godliness. For bodily exercise profits a little, but godliness is profitable for all things, having promise of the life that now is and of that which is to come. This *is* a faithful saying and worthy of all acceptance. For to this *end* we both labor and suffer reproach, because we trust in the living God, who is *the* Savior of all men, especially of those who believe. These things command and teach.

—1 Tim. 4:6-11)

We have always heard that a dog is man's best friend. This is especially true if you are physically blind. You must put your full trust in the dog to guide you through life's daily tasks.

If you are spiritually blind, however, your guide dog could be your worst enemy. You see, if you are spiritually blind, you are probably feeding your dog the wrong food. If you feed your dog the wrong food, he probably won't eat or will eat very little. He will then become hungry, weak, and disobedient and will lead you in the wrong direction. The dog will be looking for something to satisfy its appetite. If you do not feed your guide dog right, you are probably not feeding yourself right, either. If that is so, your dog becomes just like its master, hungry and disobedient.

How will you regain control of your dispirited guide dog? You must begin by filling yourself with the right food. This, in turn, will feed your guide dog and strengthen it so that your dog will be able to guide you through life's trials.

The food you need is the Word of God. You must have a daily diet of the Word. The great thing is that you don't have to worry about feeding yourself too much. It is low in fat but high in blessing. So eat up and don't give up! Feed yourself daily!

Handicap Access

"Let not your heart be troubled; you believe in God, believe also in Me. In My Father's house are many mansions; if *it were* not *so*, I would have told you. I go to prepare a place for you. And if I go and prepare a place for you, I will come again and receive you to Myself; that where I am, *there* you may be also. And where I go you know, and the way you know."
Thomas said to Him, "Lord, we do not know where You are going, and how can we know the way?"
Jesus said to him, "I am the way, the truth, and the life. No one comes to the Father except through Me."

—John 14:1-6

We sinners are all handicapped in the sense that we cannot get to God by our own power. We need an access ramp that only He can provide. Who is this access ramp? It is Jesus. He is the only access we have to the Father (above). Jesus provided a way when there was no way. He provided the way through the cross. Jesus died so that we could have full access to the Father.

If we look at most churches, they provide a few parking spaces up front for the handicap and senior citizens. If you think about it, however, the whole parking lot should be marked with handicap spaces. We are all handicapped spiritually and need help in our walk. We need someone to lean on or carry us, because we cannot do it in our own strength. We must look to Jesus in these times. He will pick us up. He will carry us when we need it the most. We must trust and obey Him. He will carry us through all our trials—not around them but through them. If He took us around our trials, we would never learn from them. If we don't learn, we will keep falling into the same sin and will not be able to grow.

Before all this can take place, however, we need to repent of our sins and ask Jesus to forgive us. Our biggest handicap is admitting we are sinners and have sinned against God. He already knows what we have done. Do not try to hide it from Him. He sees everything and knows all.

Do not be an Adam or Eve! Come out from behind that fig tree and expose your sin. You cannot hide from God, so come out, and He will be just and will forgive you. Have a great day and don't eat the apples!

Handy Man Special

No weapon formed against you shall prosper,
And every tongue *which* rises against you in judgment
You shall condemn.
This *is* the heritage of the servants of the LORD,
And their righteousness *is* from Me,"
Says the LORD.

—Isa. 54:17

The day we enter into this world, our life is like a new piece of property. We are new, fresh, and have great potential. Who or what we allow access to our properties determines the type of value it will have. It's one of the greatest investments out there, it just depends what we invest into it and how much time we invest in it.

If you let the world invest in your property, it will come in, build you up, and build up a trust. Then it will use that trust to deceive you for its benefit. Then it will tear you down. The world does not have your best interest in mind; it is only interested in owning you in order to increase its worldly wealth by using you for its success. If you let the world control your property, the world will take and use it, then run it into the ground. It will force your property into a foreclosure and, unfortunately, will still have some control over you. Then it will sell you to the highest bidder, and the cycle will start all over again.

The world will think it has won, but what it doesn't realize is the highest bidder has all the profits and has your best interest in mind. The people of the world cannot see it because of their greed, which blinds them to the truth. The truth is that your new owner can give you a new lease on life, turn your property around, and make it more profitable than it ever was or ever would have been in the hands of the world. Jesus can take the old and make it new again.

As it was in the beginning, it shall be in the end. The Bible says, "For God did not send His Son into the world to condemn the world, but that the world through Him might be saved" (John 3:17). Even though the world might condemn you, Jesus will always be there to redeem you. Jesus came into the world to save you, forgive you, and take away your sins. All you have to do is repent of your sins, ask Jesus to come live inside your heart, and have the faith of a mustard seed. Jesus died on the cross on Calvary, and the blood He shed was more than enough to cover your sins.

Next time you feel evicted, get convicted, run to the cross, and repent of your sins. Have a great day, and God bless!

Harboring Pain

My son, give attention to my words;
Incline your ear to my sayings.
Do not let them depart from your eyes;
Keep them in the midst of your heart;
For they *are* life to those who find them,
And health to all their flesh.
Keep your heart with all diligence,
For out of it *spring* the issues of life.

—Prov. 4:20-23

How clean is your harbor? Most Christians' harbors look inviting, clean, and safe on the surface. What lurks below the surface, however, tells a different story.

When Jesus saves us, we are supposed to release everything to Him, but often our sinful nature does not allow us to do this. We hold onto past hurts and unforgiveness inflicted upon us at one time during our lives. If we don't release the useless things from the past, how are we going to release the junk that comes upon us every day? If we don't let go of it, what we hold onto will block our harbors. Then it will become uninviting to the people around us. We may fall out of fellowship, become depressed, and then begin harboring more sin until our waters become stagnant. When the tide goes out, all our sin becomes exposed.

Next time the tide, which is Jesus, comes in; we need to ask Jesus to clean us up. He will dredge up the sins in our harbors and wash them away, never to have them return to us. In this way, the channels to our harbors will always be clear. When they are clear, we can talk to God through them.

Let us keep our harbors clean and our channels unblocked. Every time the tide goes out, release everything in your harbor to Jesus. Stop harboring your sins, and have a great day!

Hardware "Story"

Servants, *be* submissive to *your* masters with all fear, not only to the good and gentle, but also to the harsh. For this *is* commendable, if because of conscience toward God one endures grief, suffering wrongfully. For what credit *is it* if, when you are beaten for your faults, you take it patiently? But when you do good and suffer, if you take it patiently, this *is* commendable before God. For this you were called, because Christ also suffered for us, leaving us an example, that you should follow His steps:

"Who committed no sin,
Nor was deceit found in His mouth;"

who, when He was reviled, did not revile in return; when He suffered, He did not threaten, but committed *Himself* to Him who judges righteously; who Himself bore our sins in His own body on the tree, that we, having died to sins, might live for righteousness—by whose stripes you were healed. For you were like sheep going astray, but have now returned to the Shepherd and Overseer of your souls.

—1 Peter 2:18-25

Now, since Jesus saved me, every time I visit a hardware store and I walk up and down the aisles through the different sections, I see things differently. For example, when I'm in the lumber section, I look at lumber differently. I don't see lumber. I see the wood that made the cross where Jesus died on for my sins. When I walk down the section where the nails are, I think of the nails that pierced the hands and feet of my Savior, Jesus Christ. When I walk through the tools section and see the hammers, they remind me of my sin, which is the hammer that drove the nails into the hands and feet of Jesus. As I walk through the last section, I see the rope they used to lift the cross in place.

You may think, *This sure sounds like a sad story,* but the story is not over. It is just the beginning! That's right! Even though Jesus died on the cross on Calvary, it was not the end. It was the end of the beginning. Jesus died, was buried, and three days later He rose from the dead. Jesus defeated death, hell, and the grave, and He did this all for you! Who in the world would do this for me? There is no one but Jesus Christ! We know that is possible only through the power of the almighty God, who sent His only Son, Jesus, to earth to be born of a virgin, have the sins of the world dumped on His shoulders, and be crucified on our behalf. His death gave us the hope of salvation. All we have to do to receive it is to believe in the death, burial, and resurrection of Jesus, then ask Him to come and reside in our heart, forgive us of our sins, change us, and make us new people the only way He can, which is through the blood He shed on the cross.

Next time you visit the hardware store, walk down the aisles and see what Jesus did for you. You will never be the same again. God bless, and have a great day!

He Hauls

"The Spirit of the Lord God is upon Me,
Because the LORD has anointed Me
To preach good tidings to the poor;
He has sent Me to heal the brokenhearted,
To proclaim liberty to the captives,
And the opening of the prison to *those who are* bound;
To proclaim the acceptable year of the LORD,
And the day of vengeance of our God;
To comfort all who mourn,
To console those who mourn in Zion,
To give them beauty for ashes,
The oil of joy for mourning,
The garment of praise for the spirit of heaviness;
That they may be called trees of righteousness,
The planting of the LORD, that He may be glorified."

—Isa. 61:1-3

When we move from one place to another, we try to leave stuff behind so the load we carry will be light. This includes things we brought into our lives, which burden us and hold us back. We should have left this stuff behind the last time we moved but we took it with us, anyway.

Often, the reason we move in the first place is to get away from something that is burdening us, but we continue carrying the burdens from one destination to another. It's as if we never left our first destination. If we are ever going to leave our past behind us, we must unpack before we start packing. We must unload all our burdens, carry them out to the curb, and call for a special trash (sin) pickup. We need someone to come into our lives and carry away the sins we collected from our past but have never released.

We can't do this in our own strength. We are too weak and need someone to pick us up and remove us from our sins. We must cry out to Jesus. Jesus can take our past sin and haul it away with the blood He shed on Calvary. He will never bring it up again.

Stop storing sin in your heart. Let Jesus come in and clean it out. Have a great day, and God bless!

Heirloom

Do not lay up for yourselves treasures on earth, where moth and rust destroy and where thieves break in and steal; but lay up for yourselves treasures in heaven, where neither moth nor rust destroys and where thieves do not break in and steal. For where your treasure is, there your heart will be also.

—Matt. 6:19-21

While growing up, our mother, father or grandparents may have handed down stuff to us—belongings that really mean something to our family or tell a story about them. It is a living history lesson that our family passed on from generation to generation.

Often, however, those items handed down to one family member and not to the other can start an argument. Time and again, it tears a family apart. When this happens, neither side wins. Unfortunately, the future generations will lose out. It is almost as if two branches die and fall from your family tree. These two branches are like missing pages from a history book. Imagine that your family tree from this point on will cease to grow, its growth stunted because of the fighting and pain passed down to future generations.

It amazes me that a worldly item could cause so much of a problem. Unfortunately, the sad thing is that I can see this happening in my family after my parents pass on. I could care less if I receive anything from my parent's estate. I have memories and they are enough for me. My family is not perfect, but if you know one that is perfect, let me know. Sadly, there are people in my family who have not spoken a word to each other in years over something that happened over a decade ago.

I am the blessed one. I am the only one who can still talk to everyone in my family. Of course, I say that sarcastically. It is hard being the mediator. Ever since Jesus saved me on October 7, 2001, however, I look at worldly things for what they are—things. The greatest gift I ever received came from above, not from the world. It was a gift sent down from heaven in the form of a child. This child lived a sinless life and then gave up His life for us so that we could receive the gift of eternal life. This gift is free and available to anyone who wants to receive it. There is no will appointing it to just one person. Nothing can hold it up in the courts! It is the will of God that everyone receives it.

How can I receive it? All you have to do is repent of your sins and ask Jesus to come into your heart to be your Lord and personal Savior and change your life forever. Remember, the tree from which this gift came can never be broken, because it is the tree of life and will never perish. Have a great day, and stop barking up the wrong tree! God bless!

Hell Bound

And every priest stands ministering daily and offering repeatedly the same sacrifices, which can never take away sins. But this Man, after He had offered one sacrifice for sins forever, sat down at the right hand of God, from that time waiting till His enemies are made His footstool. For by one offering He has perfected forever those who are being sanctified.
But the Holy Spirit also witnesses to us; for after He had said before,
"This is the covenant that I will make with them after those days, says the LORD: I will put My laws into their hearts, and in their minds I will write them," then He adds, "Their sins and their lawless deeds I will remember no more." Now where there is remission of these, *there is* no longer an offering for sin.

—Heb. 10:11-18

Whether you like it or not, if you have never accepted Jesus Christ as your personal Lord and Savior, you are hell bound.

How can that be? I have been a member of the same church my whole life and have never missed a Sunday. I don't understand. I went to confession on a weekly basis to ask for forgiveness of my sins. I did this believing I was going to heaven because of these things. I was a good person. I did what I thought was right.

You know, we are all descendants of Adam and Eve. When they sinned in the Garden of Eden was when sin entered into the world and therefore we became sinners. Romans 5:12 and 14 says, "Therefore, just as through one man sin entered the world, and death through sin, and thus death spread to all men, because all sinned. Nevertheless, death reigned from Adam to Moses, even over those who had not sinned according to the likeness of the transgression of Adam, who is a type of Him who was to come."

The only way to escape hell is through Jesus Christ. Jesus, which is God in the flesh (1 Timothy 3:16) came into this world to save us. He came as a baby, born of a virgin by the power of God. He lived a sinless life among us for thirty-three years and then went to Calvary, where He died for our sins. He did not die for anything He did, even though many accused Him of crimes He didn't commit. The blood Jesus shed on Calvary was the atonement we needed to cover our sins, and the cross Jesus died upon provided the connection—the bridge—we need to get to God. The only way to the Father is through His Son, Jesus (John 14:6). The Bible also tells us in 1 John 4:10, "This is love: not that we loved God, but that He loved us and sent His Son as an atoning sacrifice for our sins." How can I receive this atonement to cover my sins? You must be born again. All you have to do is ask Jesus Christ to come live inside your heart, forgive you of your sins, to change you and make you a new person. That is what it means to "be saved". You must make the choice for yourself while you are still alive. No one can do it for you.

In the John 3:3-8, Jesus was speaking to Nicodemus. He said, "*Most assuredly, I say to you, unless one is born again, he cannot see the kingdom of God.*" Nicodemus said to Him, "How can a man be born when he is old? Can he enter a second time into his mother's womb and be born?" Jesus said, "*Most assuredly, I say to you, unless one is born of the water and the Spirit, he cannot enter the kingdom of God. That which is born of the flesh is flesh, and that which is born of the Spirit is spirit. Do not marvel that I said to you, 'You must be born again.' The wind blows where it wishes, and you hear the sound of it, but cannot tell where it comes from and where it goes. So is everyone who is born of the Spirit.*"

I love my pastor, but he cannot save me, but He can tell me how Jesus can save me so that I can spend eternity in heaven with Jesus. My pastor tells us all the time, "Don't come here for me. Come here for Jesus, because He will never let you down." I think my pastor's favorite quote is, "You met the pastor, but have you met the Master?" Don't be blinded by the truth. Trust Jesus and live! God bless, and have a great day!

Hero

I called on the LORD in distress;
The LORD answered me *and set me* in a broad place.
The LORD is on my side;
I will not fear.
What can man do to me?
The LORD is for me among those who help me;
Therefore I shall see *my desire* on those who hate me.
It is better to trust in the LORD
Than to put confidence in man.

—Ps. 118:5-8

Growing up, most of us had some type of hero. It might have been your father or mother, a sports player, a super hero, or a movie star. Perhaps something happened to your hero and he or she let you down. We must remember that we are all human and of the flesh and can't always be trusted.

We also have a tendency to forget about those who may look up to us. We commit sin, sometimes in a way that is irreversible in their eyes. We think more about the winning instead of the sinning. Often, our hero has been through the same circumstances we have been through or are currently going through.

We need a hero who is perfect, one who will never let us down. Does such a hero exist, and if so, where can I find this person? We must realize that because nobody in this world is perfect and never will be, this hero must be from out of this world.

I know a hero and He is definitely from out of this world, but He came into the world to save it. Many of us miss Him because the world hides Him from us. The world doesn't want us to hear the truth. Jesus came into the world to free us from the bondage of this world—bondage that blinds us and keeps us in our sinful ways. A definition of a real hero is Jesus Christ. He will never let you down, but He will pick you up. You see, a real hero will hang around for you, and that is what Jesus did. Jesus hung on a rugged cross for you. He died and shed His blood to cover your sins and the sins of the world.

Think before you choose a hero. Choose the only hero who can change your life and give you a life that will last for an eternity. Choose Jesus! Have a great day!

Hotel

Two *are* better than one,
Because they have a good reward for their labor.
For if they fall, one will lift up his companion.
But woe to him *who is* alone when he falls,
For *he has* no one to help him up.
Again, if two lie down together, they will keep warm;
But how can one be warm *alone*?
Though one may be overpowered by another, two can withstand him,
And a threefold cord is not quickly broken.

—Eccl. 4:9-12

There are many hotels throughout the United States. A hotel caters to your different needs, depending on what they are. If you need to arrange a party, they have the room for it. If you are planning a conference, they can set you up with rooms and a place to hold your meeting. On the other hand, if you are just on vacation with your family, they can handle that too.

Even though hotels are great for many good things, they can also be places where bad things can take place. A hotel room is a dangerous place for a person to be alone, even if he or she is a Christian. Unfortunately, being alone is especially dangerous if you are far away from your family and friends. When you are on your own, you become bored, and with boredom, your mind starts to wander. You begin thinking about things you wouldn't normally think. Satan likes it when we are alone and our minds start to wander. Have you heard the saying, "An idle mind is the devil's playground"? He will put thoughts in our minds that can make us do things we wouldn't normally do.

The hotel room is like being in a different realm. We seem to forget who we are and become a different person, as if somehow transformed. The devil likes to use three things. First, you have the television. This box has at least one hundred channels, most of which are full of sin and temptations. My mother used to call the television set the "boob tube." Thirty years later, the "boob tube" takes on a whole new meaning because you would never have dreamed of seeing them on television. However, if you have cable or a satellite dish, you may as well as classify it as a "boob tube," because it seems every other channel has a woman exposing herself. I am sure many of you have cable, but don't watch that stuff. However, what happens if you are by yourself? It's a tough question to answer. If you don't want to answer it, then you are probably watching it.

Another thing the devil likes to use to tempt us to sin is the computer. The computer is a great tool if it is in the right hands and with right mindset. Unfortunately, the computer is just like the television. It is also full of things that tempt us. The Internet is also a great tool, but if used behind a locked door in hotel room, it can be very dangerous. It can cause us to look at stuff we would not normally look at if we were at home and not by ourselves.

The last thing Satan might use is either drugs or alcohol. We might not drink around those you love and who know you, but what happens to you when you are away from home in that hotel room or hotel bar? The people you meet don't know the first thing about you. How are you going to act? Are you going to take that drink or drug? No one you know can see you. That is what Satan puts in your head.

All of this comes down to how strong we are in Jesus. We cannot rely on our own will or strong convictions. Jesus is where we get the strength to stop before we sin. So, if you have to be alone in hotel, prepare yourself. Ask the hotel to block specific channels on the television and stop Internet access in your room. The best way to prepare is to have an accountability partner you can call on "24/7," no matter where you are—in a hotel room, at home, or at the office. Have a great stay and don't get carried away by sin. God bless!

Hunting Season

Be sober, be vigilant; because your adversary the devil walks about like a roaring lion, seeking whom he may devour. Resist him, steadfast in the faith, knowing that the same sufferings are experienced by your brotherhood in the world. But may the God of all grace, who called us to His eternal glory by Christ Jesus, after you have suffered a while, perfect, establish, strengthen, and settle *you*. To Him *be* the glory and the dominion forever and ever. Amen.

—1 Peter 5:8-11

Hunting season comes around only once or twice a year. There may be a special hunt or a need to control a species population. Man hunts for one particular species seven days a week, 365 days a year. You would think that a species hunted to that extent would disappear from the face of the earth. As a hunter, you are probably wondering what type of species would still survive in such great numbers. I am talking about the Christian.

The world constantly tracks down Christians. The world and the world's evil ruler, Satan, are holding people captive. He uses these people as his scouts. As Satan's hunters, they hunt down their victims. They do it in packs, just like wolves following a trail to seek out the weaker of the species—and in this case, the weaker Christian. They use the weak Christians to gain access to the stronger Christians, just as the High Priest used Judas, a weak disciple, to lead him to Jesus. The world takes the weak Christians and begins feeding them lies. They slowly start building trust and a relationship with them. The weak Christians then join the pack and fall back into the ways of the world. Soon they begin howling like the wolves. Every howl is like a rumor that spreads around. Other Christians hear the rumors. They begin questioning and then seek answers to the rumors. Then they hunt for the person accused of the rumors.

Christians need to pick up the sword of the Spirit, which is the Word of God, and go hunting for the answers to their problems. They must find where the rumor originated and stop it at the source, preventing it from happening again. We need to switch roles with the world and become the hunter instead of the hunted. Our reason to go hunting should be to find lost souls. We must reach the world before the world reaches us, bags us like trophies, hangs us on the walls, and brags about how they made us fall. Instead of listening to the world boast, we Christians need to proclaim to the world about the One who hung on the cross for our sins. Jesus didn't have to hunt us down or force us to follow Him. Jesus drew us near to Him by showing His love toward us. He did this by going to the cross and dying for the penalties of our sins so that we may have eternal life.

Have a great day, go hunt for lost souls in the name of Jesus, and then give Jesus the glory. God bless!

Impressions

As in water face *reflects* face,
So a man's heart *reveals* the man.
Hell and Destruction are never full;
So the eyes of man are never satisfied.
The refining pot *is* for silver and the furnace for gold,
And a man *is valued* by what others say of him.
—Prov. 27:19-21

When you were growing up, did you ever watch your dad build something with concrete? Once your dad finished spreading the concrete, did you take a stick and write your name or put your handprint in the concrete and write the date it took place underneath it?

Imagine that God made the world out of freshly poured concrete and at the end of each day, the concrete hardened.

What impression would you leave behind? Imagine if every step you took left an impression of whom and what you are. Unfortunately, most of us wouldn't think about the impressions we left behind in the concrete at that time. After we thought about what we did, however, it would be too late to go back and smooth over those impressions, because the concrete would have already dried. Then we would have to live with those impressions we left behind for the rest of our lives.

If the world were like this, you would think before stepping into trouble, because once you step into trouble, it is hard to get out. If you are of this world, you don't really care what kind of impression you leave behind because you don't care whom you step on or what you step in. Imagine stepping into something that keeps you coming back for more. It could be self-centeredness, drugs, alcohol, or pornography. Whatever it is, if you step into it too many times, you are going to get stuck. The concrete is going to solidify around you, and you will not be able to step out of your sin. What type of impression will that leave in your life? You see, it doesn't seem to matter what kind of impression we make until someone catches us. Once caught in sin, you wonder how you are going to get rid of your concrete shoes. The only way to get rid of your concrete shoes is to repent of your sins and ask Jesus Christ to come into your life, change you, and make you a new person, as only He can.

Jesus left the greatest impressions I know. The impressions He made are on His hands and His feet, where the nails were driven and the blood flowed to cover our sins. If you are stuck and can't get free, look to Jesus and He will pull you from your sin and set you free. Do not become settled in the concrete of the world. Nail it down, instead, and live forever. God bless, and have a great day!

Impurities

"Behold, I have refined you, but not as silver;
I have tested you in the furnace of affliction.
For My own sake, for My own sake, I will do *it*;
For how should *My name* be profaned?
And I will not give My glory to another."

—Isa. 48:10-11

Before Jesus saved us, our hearts were as hard as a piece of iron. They were rigid and callous, and nothing could change or penetrate them. Our lives revolved around the things of the world. We would do anything to get ahead in the game of life. We didn't care who we hurt or how much we hurt others, because it was all about us. One day the tables turned. What you did years ago is now coming back to haunt you. The way you used to treat people is now happening to you. Someone is coming up behind you, doing the same thing you did, and that person doesn't care if he or she hurts you or anybody else.

When God created us, He created us in His own image (Genesis 1:27). He formed us out of the dust of the ground (Genesis 2:7). Although God made us in His image, our makeup is quite different. When God created us out of the dust of the earth, we also picked up the impurities of the world. This is what separates us from God—all our impurities, which is our sin. The impurities in our lives are like the impurities in a piece of iron ore mined from the earth. The only way to remove the impurities is to refine it with a fire so hot that it melts the iron. All the impurities float to the top as slag, and then the slag is removed. Once this process is complete, what was once iron is now molten steel, which is then poured into forms, which will be used for different applications.

Our lives are the same way. God can never use us in the state we are in, so the only way God can use us is if we go through a refining process. We must repent of our sins and ask Jesus Christ to come into our lives, penetrate and refine our hearts in order that He can use us for His glory. You see, the blood of Jesus shed on Calvary was the beginning of the refinement process to take away our impurities. Jesus led a sinless life for thirty-three years, lived among His people, and was tempted in every way possible by Satan. However, Jesus rejected sin and the ways of the world. Jesus is the only way to the Father. Jesus says in John 14:6, "No one comes to the Father except through Me."

Let Jesus separate you from the world, let Him take away all your impurities, and let Him iron out all your wrinkles. God bless, and have a great day!

Inside Out

So it was, when they came, that he looked at Eliab and said, "Surely the LORD's anointed *is* before Him!"
But the LORD said to Samuel, "Do not look at his appearance or at his physical stature, because I have refused him. For *the* LORD *does* not *see* as man sees; for man looks at the outward appearance, but the LORD looks at the heart."

—1 Sam. 16:6-7

When Christians look at a person, we are always trying to figure them out. Most of us do not look at what is on the inside. Our tendency is to look at the outward appearance. Unfortunately, 99 percent of the time we are dead wrong in our assumptions. The world we live in has a lot to do with this. The world places a great emphasis on the way we should look on the outside. We should not act this way. It is a form of judging. The

Bible says in Matthew 7:5, "Hypocrite! First remove the plank from your own eye, and then you will see clearly to remove the speck from your brother's eye."

When the world looks at a person, it looks to see if he or she is attractive, wealthy and has status. If they "pass," the world thinks they are the greatest person and wants to be like them, to emulate them. The world puts that person on a pedestal. Unfortunately, most of the time, the world is wrong.

We must to stop being like the world and be more like Jesus. We need to begin looking into people's hearts. I know we can't physically see a person's heart. However, we can observe the way a person acts, treats others, and if they "walk the walk." Jesus was the greatest example. He walked a perfect walk. Jesus acted from the inside out—from His heart and not from His head. Jesus showed us His heart when He went to the cross and died for our sins.

We Christians must carry our cross on a daily basis to remind us of what Jesus did for us. We need to feel the weight of the cross and remind ourselves continually of our sins that God dumped upon Jesus. Let us begin living our lives from the inside out instead of from the outside in. If we do this, the world may see and have a change of heart, instead of a change of mind. Have a great day, and God bless!

Junk Collector

Turn Yourself to me, and have mercy on me,
For I *am* desolate and afflicted.
The troubles of my heart have enlarged;
Bring me out of my distresses!
Look on my affliction and my pain,
And forgive all my sins.

—Ps. 25:16-18

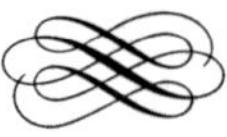

Have you ever known a junk collector, or have you ever been one? I think most of us can classify ourselves as junk collectors. I am not talking about the same junk you are probably thinking about, such as the stuff you buy and end up storing in your attic or garage for years. I am talking about the junk you hold in your heart—the junk you refuse to let go of or forgive. We all want to be forgiving, but sometimes it is too hard to forgive when someone hurts you. We hold on to this unforgiveness for so long that it begins to eat away at us like cancer. Unfortunately, we still do not release it. Our heart becomes so full of unforgiveness that bitterness takes hold. We feel that we are going to have a heart attack or fall-out.

We finally realize we need help but don't know where to find it. Unfortunately, most of us look to this world for help but end up more hurt, with more pain and unforgiveness in our hearts than before. The pain becomes so great that our hearts almost cease to keep us alive. The sad truth is that we are dying and don't even know it.

The help you need is not of this world. The help you need came to this world as a baby, born of a virgin birth, lived among us, and died for us on the cross at Calvary. We can find the help we need only in Jesus Christ. Cry out to Him. Ask Him to forgive you of your sins, which is the unforgiveness and bitterness you have in your heart. We need Jesus to cleanse us with His blood and wash us white as snow. Only He can remove all the junk, and will never bring it up again. Let us start forgiving others, tell them how they can get rid of their junk, and scrap their old lives for a new one in Jesus Christ. Don't be the "Sanford and Son" of this world. Let Jesus collect all your junk then let Him haul it away. Have a great day!

Level

"Enter by the narrow gate; for wide *is* the gate and broad *is* the way that leads to destruction, and there are many who go in by it. Because narrow *is* the gate and difficult *is* the way which leads to life, and there are few who find it."

—Matt. 7:13-14

Christians try to walk a walk that is level and upright. Unfortunately, we often lean too far one way and get off balance and then fall. If we would compare our walk to a level that a carpenter uses when he builds a house, we could learn how to keep our walk straight. When you lay it on a flat surface, the bubble in the glass rests perfectly between the two lines. This tells you that what you are leveling is perfectly straight.

If you hire a contractor to build your house, you expect him to make the walls level. Christians need to be like that bubble in the glass tube. We need to stay centered in our walk with God. It sounds easy, but attempt to walk with the level in your hands, trying to keep the bubble between the lines. It is not as easy as it sounds. Often, our walk is like that; it goes back and forth, never staying in the middle. If we could keep our lives or bubbles between the lines, we would not need Jesus.

With all the sin we have in our lives, however, that is impossible. We must seek Jesus every day by reading the Word, which is the Bible. If we do not stay in the Word, our lives will become off-centered, which could cause us to fall back into our old ways. Dig into the Word of God, and center your life on Him to enable you to walk straight and stand firm. Have a great day, and God bless!

Life Insurance

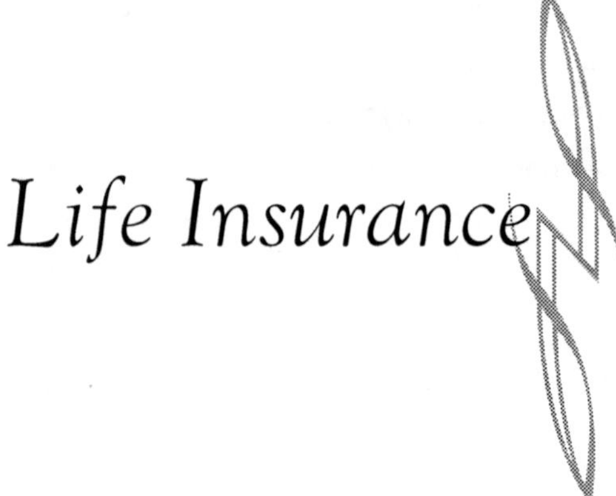

In Him also we have obtained an inheritance, being predestined according to the purpose of Him who works all things according to the counsel of His will, that we who first trusted in Christ should be to the praise of His glory.
In Him you also *trusted*, after you heard the word of truth, the gospel of your salvation; in whom also, having believed, you were sealed with the Holy Spirit of promise, who is the guarantee of our inheritance until the redemption of the purchased possession, to the praise of His glory.

—Eph. 1:11-14

How much life insurance do you have for your family? Is it enough to take care of them in a time of need when you are not around? Do they have someone they can run to and depend on? I am not talking about money, possessions, or a friend. You think they are your friend until something happens or when you need their help. I've noticed in my life that every time I've needed help moving something, such as a piece of furniture or my household belongings, everyone that you thought would jump in and help you either is too busy or makes some kind of excuse for not helping. However, when they needed your help, you were the first one there and the last one to leave.

There is only one person whom you can always count on to be there whenever you need Him. Jesus insures you in everything there is. There is no better life insurance than that found in Jesus Christ. His policy has no premiums, no increases, and no limitations. It isn't a short-term policy; it is a long-term one. Once you receive it, you cannot lose it. It doesn't cost you a dime. However, it did cost Jesus His life. We know Jesus has the best life insurance policy in heaven. He just had to wait three days for the blood work to come back. Jesus shed His blood on Calvary for our sins, and it paid for our life insurance.

Start preparing for your future. Seal it with the blood of Jesus Christ, and live life to its fullest, forever and ever. Amen!

Life or Death Sentence

Then I saw a great white throne and Him who sat on it, from whose face the earth and the heaven fled away. And there was found no place for them. And I saw the dead, small and great, standing before God, and books were opened. And another book was opened, which is *the Book* of Life. And the dead were judged according to their works, by the things which were written in the books. The sea gave up the dead who were in it, and Death and Hades delivered up the dead who were in them. And they were judged, each one according to his works. Then Death and Hades were cast into the lake of fire. This is the second death.
And anyone not found written in the Book of Life was cast into the lake of fire.

—Rev. 20:11-15

When you die or when the world comes to an end, you will stand face to face with our Creator, God! At the Great White Throne of Judgment, what type of judgment will He have for you? Will you be prepared to defend yourself? When you existed on earth, you had opportunity after opportunity to ask Jesus to come into your life and save you for eternity with Him but you said, "I am not ready yet. I am having too much fun in my sin," or, "I've got plenty of time."

Are you ready now for the sentence God has for you? He did not miss a second of your life. He knows all and sees all. On one side, God has the Lamb's Book of Life and on the other side, *He* has *His* judgment for you, and let me tell you, you do not want to be judged by the One who knows everything about you. When the judge hands down your sentence and the gavel hits the sound block, it will seem as if a trap door opens, and you will feel as if a fiery pit will swallow you up. The torment and separation from God will be forever. There will not be any appeals and no second chances. It is for eternity. You had opportunities on earth for a second chance, and probably a third and even a fourth chance, and but you did not choose to change. You chose to live a sinful life, one full of earthly pleasures. Since you chose not to change, you received what you deserved—the death penalty with no chance of parole and no chance of someone bailing you out or setting you free.

If God gave you a second chance, would you choose to live your life differently than you do now? Will you change your pending death sentence in hell into a life sentence in heaven with Jesus? Sadly, many people would not and are not willing to change, no matter how many chances they are given.

If you are reading this right now, you still have a second chance to change. Do not let this opportunity pass you by; because once you put this book down and think about it for a while, it might be too late. Please do not hesitate! My pastor always says, "Eternity is too long to be wrong." Make the right choice today, die to your sin, and live forever in eternity with Jesus. All you have to do is repent of your sins, and ask Jesus to save you, change you, and be your personal Lord and Savior. You must truly mean this with every fiber of your being. God bless, and have a great day! Choose life and be set free!

Life's a Beach

"Wash yourselves, make yourselves clean;
Put away the evil of your doings from before My eyes.
Cease to do evil,"
"Come now, and let us reason together,"
Says the LORD,
"Though your sins are like scarlet,
They shall be as white as snow;
Though they are red like crimson,
They shall be as wool."

—Isa. 1:16, 18

You can tell a lot about Christians by looking at them as a beach and seeing how white their sands are. Most of us would be ashamed to invite people to our beach and have them notice it is not as white as it used to be. We are always dragging stuff into our lives that we do not need. Stuff we are ashamed of, after the tide carries it back onto our shores. We try to bury it in the sand and we hide it out of sight, but it's not hidden. It breaks down in the sand and slowly discolors our beach—not too noticeably at first.

Unfortunately, we drag new stuff into our lives and try to keep it hidden by building sand castles to mask what is there. Soon, our once-white, sandy beach becomes brown from all the sin that either we dragged to shore or the tide washed up. The sea usually casts back the stuff washed in by the tide and carries it away by the currents. Our sinful nature, however, doesn't allow us to do that all the time. We drag so much sin onto our beach, until there is so much sin in our sands that a stench arises. Once this happens, we realize we need help.

The help we find is in our Lord Jesus Christ. He can come in, sift the sin out of our sands, and make it as white as snow. This allows us to invite people to our beach and allows them see how good God really is. God bless, and don't forget your Son screen!

Life's Signs

"And there will be signs in the sun, in the moon, and in the stars; and on the earth distress of nations, with perplexity, the sea and the waves roaring; men's hearts failing them from fear and the expectation of those things which are coming on the earth, for the powers of the heavens will be shaken. Then they will see the Son of Man coming in a cloud with power and great glory. Now when these things begin to happen, look up and lift up your heads, because your redemption draws near."

—Luke 21:25-28

Signs guide us every day, but we don't always pay attention to them. We see signs such as "Wrong Way," "One Way," "Stop," and "Dead End." These signs would really help us if we obeyed them and applied them in our daily life.

We need to learn to "Stop" before we do something that might hurt us or someone else. If only we would realize that being of this world is the "Wrong Way" to get to heaven. We must realize that being of this world always leads to a "Dead End" and there is only "One Way" to hell and "One Way" to heaven. The "One Way" to hell is being of this world and living a sin-filled life. The "One Way" and only way to heaven is repenting of your sins, surrendering your life and sinful ways to Jesus, allowing Him to save you by the blood that was shed on the cross on Calvary.

"Yield" to your sin and turn to the cross. Bypass all the U-turns, heed the "Do Not Enter" areas in your life, and stay on the "One Way" road to the cross. Have a great day, and God bless!

Limited Time Offer

Beware, brethren, lest there be in any of you an evil heart of unbelief in departing from the living God; but exhort one another daily, while it is called "*Today,*" lest any of you be hardened through the deceitfulness of sin. For we have become partakers of Christ if we hold the beginning of our confidence steadfast to the end, while it is said:

"Today, if you will hear His voice,
Do not harden your hearts as in the rebellion."

For who, having heard, rebelled? Indeed, *was it* not all who came out of Egypt, *led* by Moses? Now with whom was He angry forty years? *Was it* not with those who sinned, whose corpses fell in the wilderness? And to whom did He swear that they would not enter His rest, but to those who did not obey? So we see that they could not enter in because of unbelief.

—Heb. 3:12-19

Most of us are always trying to get the best deal in order to save ourselves the most money possible. Unfortunately, most of these deals only last for a limited time, and then the offer is over until the next one comes around. Most of these offers are not what they seem to be. There is always some catch; something they are not telling you. You don't find out until you get home and read the small print. By that time, it is too late because you have already signed the contract. It is kind of like signing your life away—you are at the mercy of the person you signed the contract with until the payment is fully paid. It's as if you sold your soul, because once you sign on the dotted line that person has you for the term of the contract. They blind you with false advertisements saying 0 percent interest for 60 months or no payments until next year. They don't tell you about the hidden costs they include in the price, which you don't notice because you think you got such a great deal.

The evil one operates the same way. He puts false thoughts in our minds that blind us from seeing things as they really are. The truth is, the evil one does have interest in you, but he does not have your best interest in mind. He doesn't tell you about the hidden cost you incur when you decide to follow him. He doesn't tell you it will cost you your life.

However, there is a way around the lies and the false teachings. The way is through Jesus Christ. He has your best interest in mind. It will not cost you a cent. However, it is for a limited time, but it comes with a lifetime guarantee. Unfortunately, time is running out, so do not wait another second, because nobody knows when this offer will expire—which is the day you leave this earth. If you act now, Jesus will throw in grace and mercy at no additional cost to you. There are no strings attached. Therefore, do not miss this opportunity. Act now, have faith, and you will never be burned again. God bless, and have a great day!

Love Letter to God

What then shall we say to these things? If God *is* for us, who *can be* against us? He who did not spare His own Son, but delivered Him up for us all, how shall He not with Him also freely give us all things? Who shall bring a charge against God's elect? *It is* God who justifies. Who *is* he who condemns? *It is* Christ who died, and furthermore is also risen, who is even at the right hand of God, who also makes intercession for us. Who shall separate us from the love of Christ? *Shall* tribulation, or distress, or persecution, or famine, or nakedness, or peril, or sword? As it is written:

"For Your sake we are killed all day long;
We are accounted as sheep for the slaughter."

Yet in all these things we are more than conquerors through Him who loved us. For I am persuaded that neither death nor life, nor angels nor principalities nor powers, nor things present nor things to come, nor height nor depth, nor any other created thing, shall be able to separate us from the love of God which is in Christ Jesus our Lord.

—Rom. 8:31-39

If you were to write a love letter to God, what would you say? How would you begin your letter? I think we all should write Him a love letter because He first loved us (1 John 4:19). He showed us His love by sending His Son, Jesus, into this world to show us we are to love one another, even our enemies. God told us of His love in the Bible in John 3:16: "For God so love the world [not just me] that He gave His only begotten Son that whosoever believeth in Him shall not perish but have everlasting life."

Where do we begin? What do we say? Where and how do we start such a letter to our God, who loves us so much? I think, instead of writing a letter on a piece of paper, we need to look deep into our hearts to see if we really do love God more than we love ourselves. God created us in His own image (Genesis 1:27). I don't know why He did what He did, but I know the image I sometimes reflect isn't God's image. It is my own selfish image, which can be quite ugly sometimes.

What we must do is to let our walk reflect our heart. Unfortunately, over the years most of us have had a kind of bypass surgery. Essentially, we have cut off the blood supply to our hearts, which is the love of Christ. By doing this, our hearts have become so hardened and cold that it hurts. With our hearts being in so much pain, it is hard to show God's love to someone who really needs to see it.

We need to reconnect our hearts to God and let His love shine through our hearts for the world to see. I think that if God could see a change in our hearts, it would be more pleasing to Him than any love letter He could receive. Have a blessed day!

MIA

But, beloved, we are confident of better things concerning you, yes, things that accompany salvation, though we speak in this manner. For God *is* not unjust to forget your work and labor of love which you have shown toward His name, *in that* you have ministered to the saints, and do minister. And we desire that each one of you show the same diligence to the full assurance of hope until the end, that you do not become sluggish, but imitate those who through faith and patience, inherit the promises.

—Heb. 6:9-12

When God first saves us, often many of us jump right in with both feet and begin serving in one or several ministries. There are those who are on fire for Jesus, telling everyone they know how God saved them, how they, too, can be saved, and how they can have a personal relationship with

Jesus Christ. They are in church whenever the doors are open and are often the first to come and the last to leave. This goes on for several years and then, for one reason or another, they quit serving, quit coming to church altogether, and fall out of fellowship with other Christians.

At first, no one notices because everyone else is so busy doing their own thing that no one misses them right away. We must go out and re-harvest those wandering souls, however, before they wander so far away from the light of the cross that they end up back in darkness. They cease to grow and then become missing in action (MIA)! We must send out the hounds of heaven to sniff out any scent of blood, the blood of Jesus Christ that saved their lost soul, and bring them back into fellowship with Him. Once they are back in fellowship, they can begin to grow again and serve in the fields. They can begin to break new ground, sow more seeds, and tend to them until they are mature and ready to aide in the harvesting for God's kingdom.

Let us be sowers of the seed and not storers. God bless, and have a great day!

Magnetism

> I say then: Walk in the Spirit, and you shall not fulfill the lust of the flesh. For the flesh lusts against the Spirit, and the Spirit against the flesh; and these are contrary to one another, so that you do not do the things that you wish. But if you are led by the Spirit, you are not under the law.
>
> —Gal. 5:16-18

Have you ever held two magnets in your hands, flipped them around, so the two same poles face each other, and tried to push them together? They wouldn't come together because of the resistance caused by the same polarity. Instead, they repel each other.

The world has two poles, north and south. The world is like a big magnet, which also rotates on the two poles. The two poles work together to make the world spin. As the world spins, it creates what we call gravity, which holds us to this world. If you took the two poles and switched them completely around, however, the world would start spinning in the opposite direction. This is kind of like our walk with God at times. We started spinning in the right direction after God saved us, but then something happens in our lives and we began spinning in the opposite direction, back into our old sinful ways. We began repelling God. Imagine if you took the north and south poles and rotated them to where the same poles faced each other. The world would blow apart.

We need to rotate our attention, which is our magnet, toward God, so we will draw closer to Him. He wants us to draw closer to Him, not away from Him. God showed His magnetism toward us by sending His Son, Jesus into this world. Then Jesus showed His magnetism toward His Father by doing God's will. He then showed His magnetism toward us by going all the way to Calvary to die for our sins on that old, rugged cross.

Do not repel the love God has shown us. We should be attracted to His love like a bee to a flower. God bless, have a great day, and magnify the Lord in your life.

Mailbox of Sin

"The heart *is* deceitful above all *things*,
And desperately wicked;
Who can know it?
I, the LORD, search the heart.
I test the mind,
Even to give every man according to his ways,
According to the fruits of his doings."

—Jer. 17:9-10

We go through life seeing so much garbage in our daily walk that it can really affect our walk if we are not strong enough and are not staying in God's Word. It is essential that we have a quiet time with God every day before we leave home. We see garbage when we wake up in the morning, as soon as we pick up the morning newspaper. We see it when we turn on the television to watch the news. If you have cable or a satellite dish, chances are, if you are weak and not in God's Word, you won't be watching the news. You will be watching something of a questionable nature, which you shouldn't be looking at. Granted, the news has enough garbage in it to begin with. When we are driving the kids to school or going to work, we see more garbage on bumper stickers and especially on those billboards with scantily clad women. Then we get to work, we find on our desk one of the most useful tools ever invented, the computer—useful, that is, if it's used for the right reasons. If we use it for the wrong reasons, it could be one of the worst inventions created. It can kill you morally and spiritually if you are not careful.

After a long day at work, we are beat. We get home and drive up to that little "tin box of sin," the mailbox. It is usually full of trash (such as explicit ads) and bills. Perhaps we should call it a trash box. Instead of having the trash delivered to us maybe, we should call the garbage man for a pickup because about 75 percent of it is trash, anyway. Maybe we could set a trashcan next to the mailbox and throw away the junk before it has a chance to get into our homes and turns our house into a garbage dump.

If you need deliverance from the garbage (sins) in your life, trust Jesus, and He will take all your garbage and return it to sender. It will not have a return address on it—so don't worry, it won't return to you. Have a great day!

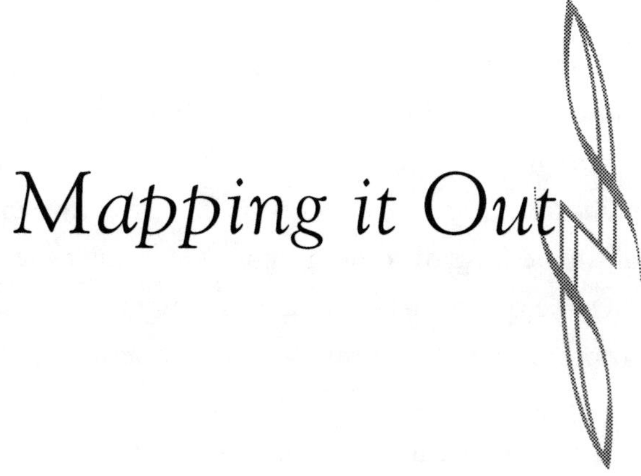

Mapping it Out

> For I know the thoughts that I think toward you, says the LORD, thoughts of peace and not of evil, to give you a future and a hope. Then you will call upon Me and go and pray to Me, and I will listen to you. And you will seek Me and find *Me*, when you search for Me with all your heart.
>
> —Jer. 29:11-13

When you looked at an atlas and all the roads that are on the map, does it overwhelm you? There are so many roads and different directions we can take and so many ways to get lost.

Our Christian walk is like a road map. There are so many roads to travel; however, we might not always choose the correct one. God gave us the ability to make decisions for ourselves. Even though we decide which way to go, God is always in control, even when we think we are. There are many ways to go and yet so many mistakes we can make. There are U-turns, dead ends, and speed limits to maintain. When traveling down the road in our Christian drive, we do not always stay in the right lane. Sometimes we drive in the left lane to pass someone; unfortunately, we also pass opportunities. Often, we exit the highway of life because of something we see. Sometimes, something on the side of the road catches our attention, which causes us to stop and take a second look. It is often something we should not be getting into. This, in turn, causes us to stay too long off the highway of life. We may find ourselves wandering down a back road—one that is not even on the map. We think the road cannot go much farther. However, after a few more twists and turns in the road, we somehow turn around in the opposite direction and cannot find our way back to the highway of life. The sun begins to set and before we know it, not only are we lost, but the night has set in. We try to follow the sun before it drops over the horizon, because it is our only hope to get back to where we should be. Unfortunately, the sun disappears over the horizon, and all hope seems lost.

However, God always supplies a way when there seems to be no way. As we have heard, the sun rises in the east and sets in the west, and the moon rises to remind us of the dawning of a new day. Joy comes in the morning (Psalm 30:5). When Jesus came into this world, He also traveled many roads, but He was never distracted or lost. He had His life mapped out, just as we do! He came to this world for one purpose—to save us. Jesus never lost sight of His Father's will. Jesus faced many temptations in His thirty-three years but through His travels, He never sinned. He took the road that led to Calvary. He knew His purpose in life was to die for the sins of the world. He nailed it down, once and for all. Although he could have taken many detours, He stayed on the road to Calvary.

Imagine if Jesus had taken a detour right before He got to Calvary. Where would we be today? Think about it for a minute. You think we have it bad now, but imagine not being able to make a decision that could change your destination and your life forever. Imagine if all we had to look forward to was going to hell. What kind of life would we lead? Not a very promising one, I assure you. All hope would be lost. However, thank God, Jesus did His Father's will, which gave us the chance and the hope to become children of God by accepting His Son as our personal Lord and Savior.

So, let us pursue the map that God gave us to follow. It is full of instructions that will always lead us in the right direction. The map is the Holy Bible. Read it. You will be amazed where it will lead you. Keep your eyes on the Son so you won't get lost! Have a great day, and God bless!

Most Wanted

But what does it say? "*The word is near you, in your mouth and in your heart*" (that is, the word of faith which we preach): that if you confess with your mouth the Lord Jesus and believe in your heart that God has raised Him from the dead, you will be saved. For with the heart one believes unto righteousness, and with the mouth confession is made unto salvation. For the Scripture says, "*Whoever believes on Him will not be put to shame.*" For there is no distinction between Jew or Greek, for the same Lord over all is rich to all who call upon Him. For "*whoever calls on the name of the LORD shall be saved.*"

—Rom. 10:8-13

Have you ever seen the show *America's Most Wanted*? Have you seen the Old Western television shows where the Most Wanted posters are hanging outside the sheriff's office and all over town? At the bottom, they say, "Wanted Dead or Alive."

They also state the reward amount if that person is caught and brought in for judgment.

Imagine that heaven and hell used wanted posters. The posters in heaven would read: "Wanted Alive: Rewards are waiting in heaven for the person who seeks Jesus, is a witness to My people in this world, and delivers them from death to life with the power given to them through Jesus Christ." If God also placed the same wanted posters found in heaven within our hearts, we could see into our hearts and know who will live for eternity and who will die and spend eternity in hell and torment. However, that shouldn't matter. We should be a witness to everyone.

Of course, the wanted posters in hell would be different. There would not be any posters in hell for worldly people. People of the world are not on Satan's most wanted list because Satan already has them. He doesn't have time to waste on souls he already has. Why should Satan waste time putting up posters for someone he already has? The wanted posters in hell would be for those who accepted the call of salvation, those who want to be different, and those who follow Jesus and not the ways of the world. The posters in hell would probably read: "Wanted Dead or Alive: People who follow Jesus Christ, people who think they can be saved by the blood of Jesus, people who spread the gospel of Jesus Christ throughout the world." Satan says, "These are the people I want to bring down with me."

We tend to forget that once you know that God truly saved you, that your salvation is permanent. However, Satan does not want you to have the victory and joy of your salvation. He will remind you constantly of your past and try to take away your joy and make you forget about the future you have with Jesus. Satan wants you back, but he cannot have you because what goes up stays up and what goes down stays down. God showed us that when He cast Satan out of heaven, down to earth, where he has been ever since. On the other hand, at the right hand of God is seated His Son, Jesus. Once He went up, He stayed up. He will come down to earth one last time to take His children home.

Are you going to be ready to go up and stay up or go down and stay down? The decision is yours. Make the right one! Have a great day!

Nails

And you, being dead in your trespasses and the uncircumcision of your flesh, He has made alive together with Him, having forgiven you all trespasses, having wiped out the handwriting of requirements that was against us, which was contrary to us. And He has taken it out of the way, having nailed it to the cross. Having disarmed principalities and powers, He made a public spectacle of them, triumphing over them in it.

—Col. 2:13-15

Have you noticed how important nails are and have been throughout the ages? Nails hold together the house we live in. Nails hold together the table on which we eat our meals. Nails hold up all the pictures and stuff we hang on our walls. Nails hold together the furniture we sit on.

Have you ever wondered what holds you together? If you depend on the world to hold you together, good luck! The world is only out to use you. Once it is through with you, it will dispose of you like useless garbage. However, we have to remember that God does not make any junk. If we are of this world, we don't realize this and we become trapped into believing we are useless garbage. We lie in our own stench, while our lives rot away until the smell becomes as bad as a compost pile. Then, we just want to lie down and die.

At some point, however, the sweet smell of roses fertilized by the compost of our sinful lives awakens us, and we realize there is hope. That hope is Jesus Christ. It was He who died on the cross held together with nails. They nailed Jesus to the cross with three nails. Jesus wants us to know and believe that all things are possible through Him, if we trust in Him and Him alone.

Next time you hammer a nail, just remember how that nail saved your life. God bless!

New Owner

This I say, therefore, and testify in the Lord, that you should no longer walk as the rest of the Gentiles walk, in the futility of their mind, having their understanding darkened, being alienated from the life of God, because of the ignorance that is in them, because of the blindness of their heart; who, being past feeling, have given themselves over to lewdness, to work all uncleanness with greediness.

But you have not so learned Christ, if indeed you have heard Him and have been taught by Him, as the truth is in Jesus: that you put off, concerning your former conduct, the old man which grows corrupt according to the deceitful lusts, and be renewed in the spirit of your mind, and that you put on the new man which was created according to God, in true righteousness and holiness.

—Eph. 4:17-24

I was driving home from work the other day, when I looked to my left and saw a sign at a car dealership, which read: "New Owner." That got me to thinking. I have a new owner in my life and His name is Jesus Christ. He bought me with a price, which is the blood He shed on the cross at Calvary. It didn't cost me anything, but it cost Him everything. My New Owner has given me a new lease on life—a lease that has been written in the *Lamb's Book of Life*. It is a lease for eternity.

My former owner, Satan, was so upset when I moved out before my lease was up. He began to tell me, "If you ever return…," but I stopped him before he could finish. I told him, "I will never return to my old ways. You may trip me up and even knock me down, but with the power that is in the blood of Jesus Christ, I will get up and prevail over anything you throw at me. I've got the victory!" He went back to hell where he belongs.

If you are looking for a new owner, look to the One who can extend your lease on life for an eternity—Jesus Christ. He can take your old lease, which was a lease from hell, terminate it, cover your sins with His blood, and give you a new lease on life. Let Jesus be your New Owner and Savior. God bless, and have a great day!

No Respect

Therefore if *there is* any consolation in Christ, if any comfort of love, if any fellowship of the Spirit, if any affection and mercy, fulfill my joy by being like-minded, having the same love, *being* of one accord, of one mind. *Let* nothing *be done* through selfish ambition or conceit, but in lowliness of mind let each esteem others better than himself.

Let each of you look out not only for his own interests, but also for the interests of others. Let this mind be in you which was also in Christ Jesus, who, being in the form of God, did not consider it robbery to be equal with God, but made Himself of no reputation, taking the form of a bondservant, *and* coming in the likeness of men. And being found in appearance as a man, He humbled Himself and became obedient to *the point of* death, even the death of the cross. Therefore God also has highly exalted Him and given Him the name which is above every name, that at the name of Jesus every knee should bow, of those in heaven, and of those on earth, and

> those under the earth, and *that* every tongue should confess that Jesus Christ *is* Lord, to the glory of God the Father.
>
> —Phil. 2:1-11

Christians treat God like a waiter or a personal server at a fast food restaurant. We place our order or request, and then we wait impatiently while our server gets our order ready. When we finally receive it, we check to make sure our server got the order correct. We get frustrated and upset with the server, who has to stand there and take the humiliation in front of all his coworkers.

The world says the customer is always right. This is true if you are of this world. If you are a Christian, however, you should not act this way. Handle the situation with patience and longsuffering. Let it be a testimony to the person who gave you the wrong order. Let him take note of it and try to live by your example.

If we are truly Christian, we know we should serve God because of what His Son, Jesus, showed us during His time here on earth. Jesus was the greatest example of a servant. He showed us when He came to earth to live among us for thirty-three years and gave His life to die on the cross on Calvary for our sins.

We need to rethink our position and realize it is really God's position. We need to start taking our orders from God, instead of giving orders to God. Often in our prayer life, we ask God for something and when we don't get what we want, we wonder why God did not answer our request. What we don't realize is that God did answer our prayer request, but we are just too blind to see that. God knows what we need and don't need. So, open your eyes and start counting your blessings. Then you will realize God does answer prayers, just not always the way you expect.

I thank God that His ways are not my ways (Isaiah 55:8). Next time you ask God for something, ask Him not what He can do for you but what you can do for Him. If you begin doing God's will and not yours, He will bless you beyond your greatest expectations. Go bless yourself today by following God's will for your life. Have a great day!

P.O.W.

> Do not love the world or the things in the world. If anyone loves the world, the love of the Father is not in him. For all that is in the world—the lust of the flesh, the lust of the eyes, and the pride of life—is not of the Father but is of the world. And the world is passing away, and the lust of it; but he who does the will of God abides forever.
>
> —1 John 2:15-17

When I mention P.O.W., most people will think of a prisoner of war and relate it to the Vietnam War, which lasted fifteen years. There was no real winner, just a bunch of lost lives. However, since God created man, woman, and then the family, we have been at war with Satan ever since. Yes, we have been at battle for thousands of years. We have allowed more people to die and go to hell than any war has ever killed or ever will kill.

However, what I am trying to get across to all believers in Jesus Christ is that we have so many P.O.W.s right here in our hometown. They are the people we work with, people in our own families, and even people in our very own church. I call them "prisoners of the world." Yes, the world! We have so many people relying on themselves and other people to get them through life. They think that all they have is each other, which will get them nowhere. It is like the blind leading the blind. They will never have enough worldly possessions to satisfy their needs. They think they are happy, but something is missing deep inside, and they don't know what it is, where to find it, or how much it will cost.

That is where we come in. We are P.O.W.s ourselves, but P.O.W.s of a different kind. We are "people of the Word." We need to be out there spreading the Word of God to the world. The gospel of Jesus Christ saved us. We must spread it to all nations. We need to tell them how much God loves the world He created. "For God so loved the world that He gave His only begotten Son, Jesus Christ, who died for our sins that whoever believes in Him shall not perish but will have everlasting life" (John 3:16). We need to be good stewards of the Word and not keep it to ourselves. Let's go free the P.O.W.s in Jesus' name! Amen!

Past Due

I planted, Apollos watered, but God gave the increase. So then neither he who plants is anything, nor he who waters, but God who gives the increase. Now he who plants and he who waters are one, and each one will receive his own reward according to his own labor. For we are God's fellow workers; you are God's field, you are God's building. According to the grace of God which was given to me, as a wise master builder I have laid the foundation, and another builds on it. But let each one take heed how he builds on it. For no other foundation can anyone lay than that which is laid, which is Jesus Christ. Now if anyone builds on this foundation with gold, silver, precious stones, wood, hay, straw, each one's work will become clear; for the Day will declare it, because it will be revealed by fire; and the fire will test each one's work, of what sort it is. If anyone's work which he has built on it endures, he will receive a reward. If anyone's work is burned, he will suffer loss; but he himself will be saved, yet so as through fire.

—1 Cor. 3:6-15

If you are a Christian and God saved you several years ago but you haven't found a ministry to serve in yet, don't you think you are past due? Once we are saved, we should be motivated to serve, to be a witness for Jesus Christ, to show others what Jesus has done in our lives, and to tell them what Jesus can do in their lives. Imagine if Jesus never came to earth to live with us to show us His love and be an example of a servant. Where would we be today?

Jesus showed His service for us by going to Calvary and dying on the cross for our sins. We owe Jesus everything, but we can never repay Him for His sacrifice. All Jesus asks us to do is go tell the world about Him, and tell others how He can save them and have a personal relationship with Him. Yes, that is many people to reach! All you have to do is walk out your front door. There is your world. If you tell one person, the news about Jesus will spread like rumors. I am not saying Jesus is a rumor; Jesus is definitely a fact. If you would read the book of facts, your Bible, you would know this. Why are you afraid to tell someone the truth, when you find it so easy to tell a lie?

Let us start serving and spreading the truth we have in Christ Jesus and stop listening to the lies Satan throws at us. God bless, and have a great day!

Piñata

When He called all the multitude to *Himself,* He said to them, "Hear Me, everyone, and understand: There is nothing that enters a man from outside which can defile him; but the things which come out of him, those are the things that defile a man. If anyone has ears to hear, let him hear!

When He had entered a house away from the crowd, His disciples asked Him concerning the parable. So He said to them, "Are you thus without understanding also? Do you not perceive that whatever enters a man from outside cannot defile him, because it does not enter his heart but his stomach, and is eliminated, *thus* purifying all foods? And He said, "What comes out of a man, that defiles a man. For from within, out of the heart of men, proceed evil thoughts, adulteries, fornications, murders, thefts, covetousness, wickedness, deceit, lewdness, an evil eye, blasphemy, pride, foolishness. All these evil things come from within and defile a man."

—Mark 7:14-23

Before Jesus saved us, we could compare our lives to a piñata. We hang around suspended by a string, swinging from side to side. The world fills us up with worldly things that seem as sweet as candy at that moment, but over time, the sweetness disappears, leaving behind a bitter taste. Then, with the bitterness inside us, we tend to become bitter to those who love us the most. Our hearts become hard and calloused and, with all the bitterness we have in our hearts, we tend to fall into our own little world. This where Satan wants us to be—alone, hurt, and vulnerable to where he can move in and take up residence in our minds and control our lives.

Satan, the great deceiver, will move in and begin to corrupt our thoughts. He puts junk in our heads that will eventually end up in our hearts, causing us to fall deeper into our sinful ways and inflict more pain and more hurt. Our sins engulf us so much that we think we will split at the seams. That is when the attacks really begin. The people of the world move in and start beating us down even more with a big stick, trying to burst us open and expose what is in our hearts (sin) to everyone. It's like a big party to the world. Thank goodness, however, they are blind to their sinful ways by a blindfold, which is the world they live in. It misses more than it hits us because of the sinful state of its intoxication, which impairs its judgment.

Eventually, we will be hit one time too many and will burst wide open. All that is inside of us will spill out for the entire world to see. Our sin to the world is as candy is to a child or milk to a baby, because the world thrives on sin.

We want to leave the sin that binds us to this world, but we do not have the strength to cut the strings. We need to look beyond our sin and look to the cross, where Jesus died for our sins. He was beaten, spit at, and mocked. When they nailed Him to the cross, His blood spilled out to cover our sins. Does that sound familiar? You were beaten, but all that spilled out of you was sin.

The difference between Jesus and us is that He led a sinless life. He who knew no sin became sin for us (2 Corinthians 5:21). So if you have never asked Jesus to come into your life and forgive you of your sins, let me ask you one question: where do you want to spend eternity? Do you like it hot? Well, if you have never asked Jesus into your life, prepare yourself to burn. It is so simple that people miss it. They try too hard, when all it takes is to surrender your life to Jesus and ask Him to forgive you of all your sins. Stop getting beaten up by the world, and give your life to Jesus. Have a great day, and God bless!

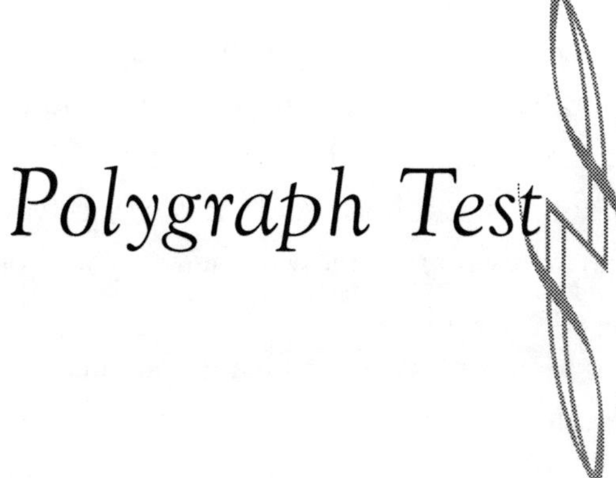

Polygraph Test

O LORD, You have searched me and known *me*.
You know my sitting down and my rising up;
You understand my thought afar off.
You comprehend my path and my lying down,
And are acquainted with all my ways.
For *there is* not a word on my tongue,
But behold, O LORD, You know it altogether.
You have hedged me behind and before,
And laid Your hand upon me.
Such knowledge *is* too wonderful for me;
It is high, I cannot *attain* it.

—Ps. 139:1-6

Imagine that the only way into heaven when you died was to take a polygraph test. It's somewhat scary if you think about it. How could you lie, when the one giving you the test is God

Himself? He knows everything about you, from the day you where born to the day you will die. He even knew you before He created the world. The Bible says, "...just as He chose us in Him before the foundation of the world..." (Ephesians 1:4). He hasn't missed a thing you did or didn't do. So, if you knew about this test, how would this change your life from the way you are living right now to the way you should start living from this day forward?

Most of us would change our perspective of the way we should be living. In today's world, unfortunately, it would be a lot harder for us to change because the world has become so corrupt that it has blinded our eyes and has brought deafness to our ears and hardness to our hearts. We have allowed the corruption to continue for so long that it has made us look the other way so we can't see it, and cover our ears so we can't hear it. It has hardened our hearts so much that we don't feel it anymore.

If this test were the difference between going to heaven or hell, wouldn't you try to change? You cannot do it by yourself. I know that because we are all sinners and liars. The only way to the Father is through His Son, Jesus, who took the polygraph test for us. Jesus is the only one who would pass the test because He is the only one who has never sinned or told a lie. How did He do this? He came to earth, lived a perfect life, and died for us on the cross at Calvary. He passed the test but He did not pass the cross. He went all the way to the cross for you and for me.

All you have to do to receive Jesus is to repent of your sin and ask Him to come into your life and change your heart, and begin living for Him instead of yourself. God bless, and have a great day!

Real or Make Believe

"Thus says the LORD, the King of Israel,
And his Redeemer, the LORD of hosts:
'I *am* the First and I *am* the Last;
Besides Me *there is* no God.
And who can proclaim as I do?
Then let him declare it and set it in order for Me,
Since I appointed the ancient people.
And the things that are coming and shall come,
Let them show these to them.
Do not fear, nor be afraid;
Have I not told you from that time, and declared *it?*
You *are* My witnesses.
Is there a God besides Me?
Indeed *there is* no other Rock;
I know not *one*.' "

—Isa. 44:6-8

What type of God do you serve? Do you serve the one and only God or a make-believe god? Are there facts backing your god or is your god made up? Did your god come down to earth to be born of a virgin? Did your god live among his people to show them how they should live and love one another? Can your god do miracles, such as raise people from the dead, free his people, who were in bondage for 400 years, and lead them to a land he promised them and, in doing so, parted the Red Sea and placed them on dry ground? Most of all, did your god hang on a cross, have six-inch nails driven through his hands and his feet, die on that cross for your sins, be buried, and then, three days later, rise from the dead? Does your god live in your heart? Will he come back at an appointed time given to him only by his father saying, "Son go get your children and bring them home"?

My God can do all of the above, and it is backed by the Bible—the Word of God, written by God for *His* children to follow and live by. Can your god do any of the above miracles? If he can't, you should stop make believing and start believing in the God who can change your life. If you believe in the god you are trusting in now, he might make life in this world look great, but once this world ends, so does your life.

Where are you placing your trust? Are you placing it in your job, money, worldly possessions, the stock market, the bottle, drugs, food, family, and friends? If any of these things consume your time, thoughts, and energy, you have elevated it to the level of a god in your life. Start trusting the one and only God who will fulfill all the promises He has made, the One who will provide for your needs, and the only One who can fill the void in your heart (life). Choose wisely, live forever, and stay out of the heat. God bless, and have a great day!

Recyclable Soul

"You are the salt of the earth; but if the salt loses its flavor, how shall it be seasoned? It is then good for nothing but to be thrown out and trampled underfoot by men.
You are the light of the world. A city that is set on a hill cannot be hidden. Nor do they light a lamp and put it under a basket, but on a lampstand, and it gives light to all *who are* in the house. Let your light so shine before men, that they may see your good works and glorify your Father in heaven.

—Matt. 5:13-16

You can compare a person's life to a bottle of soda pop. We begin our lives full of fizz and color, and we come across as very sweet and having great taste. As we age, however, we become more in tune with the things around us. We realize we are all different. Some of us are not as sweet as others are. Some of us have better taste than others do—at least we think so. There are many different flavors.

As we venture into the world, however, we find out there are many good and bad things a soda can do in the world. For instance, if you are a good soda, you could work in an ice cream shop, make floats, and make others around you very happy. You could be a good soda gone bad if you allow yourself to mix with alcohol. You make others around you feel happy, but the next morning they find that their happiness was only temporary. Their happiness turns into depression, they lose their fizz for life, their taste goes flat, and they feel worthless. They want to pour their life down the drain and call it quits. Yet again, they mix with the wrong crowd and begin mixing themselves with alcohol. Once again, they feel happy until they wake up. Because they spill their insides too many times, their lives become transparent. Their friends can see right through them to the real person inside the bottle.

Your friends desert you—at least, you thought they were your friends. Then they kick you to the curb, and the last of your dignity spills onto the street and washes down the sewer. You feel as if your life is over. You feel like useless garbage headed to the dump.

However, when all hope seems lost—it is not. We must empty ourselves to see our true self. We get so full of ourselves that sometimes we think we can take care of our problems on our own. However, once we become empty, that is when the One who created us can use us. Through His Son, Jesus Christ, all things are possible (Matthew 19:26). Let us empty ourselves, so the blood of Jesus Christ can recycle us. Pop your top and empty yourself, so the light of Jesus can shine through. God bless!

Remote Control

For the wrath of God is revealed from heaven against all ungodliness and unrighteousness of men, who suppress the truth in unrighteousness, because what may be known of God is manifest in them, for God has shown *it* to them. For since the creation of the world His invisible *attributes* are clearly seen, being understood by the things that are made, *even* His eternal power and Godhead, so that they are without excuse, because, although they knew God, they did not glorify *Him* as God, nor were thankful, but became futile in their thoughts, and their foolish hearts were darkened. Professing to be wise, they became fools, and changed the glory of the incorruptible God into an image made like corruptible man—and birds and four-footed animals and creeping things.

Therefore God also gave them up to uncleanness, in the lusts of their hearts, to dishonor their bodies among themselves, who exchanged the truth of God for the lie, and worshiped and served the creature rather than the Creator, who is blessed forever. Amen.

—Rom. 1:18-25

Have you ever lost the remote control to your TV set and found it between the cushions of your couch, along with stale potato chips and loose change? Most families have at least one remote control, if not two or more and they can never find the one they need when they need it. Unfortunately, when most families today need to find their family members, they can usually find them in front of the TV.

Your kids are playing video games, your husband is watching the sports channel, and your wife is catching up on the latest soap opera. Just as the remote gets lost in the cushion of the couch, we, as a family, are lost in the world. You can never find us where we are supposed to be. Where should you be? Well, are you a Christian? If you are, you need to get out of that recliner, drop to your knees, and ask God to forgive you for worshiping another god instead of God the Father who sent His Son, Jesus, to die for your sins.

Who is this other god? It is your television. You have been spending more time with it than with God—the God who saved you and gave you the ability to watch TV in the first place. God did not intend for us to use our eyes to watch TV all the time—men lusting over the next commercial of scantily clad women or cheerleaders, and women lusting over the next hot soap opera star. No wonder this world is so corrupt with the junk we have allowed to infiltrate our homes.

Even the junk we let our children watch is full of so much violence. It amazes me what the networks deem as appropriate for our children to watch. However, we cannot blame the networks for what our kids our watching. We have no one to blame but ourselves. Because the networks do not live in our homes, we have control of the remote. They do not! God should have control over our lives.

Do not be so remote from the One who loves you more than your own family, and give the control back to God. Have a blessed day!

Rent-a-Sinner

As for me, I will call upon God,
And the LORD shall save me.
Evening and morning and at noon
I will pray, and cry aloud,
And He shall hear my voice.
He has redeemed my soul in peace from
The battle *that was* against me,
For there were many against me.

—Ps. 55:16-18

Christians try to live and walk the walk that will bring glory to God. The world makes this very difficult when temptations are so prevalent in our everyday walk. Satan uses this to his advantage. Satan knows what it will take to make us fall back into our sinful ways.

When we sin, we are not pleasing God, and that is what Satan wants. He wants us to forget where God has brought us. He also wants us to stumble and fall so that we will live a defeated life. When we feel defeated, Satan receives the victory. We have to stop and think before we jump, because if we jump before we think, nine times out of ten it leads to defeat. It is as if Satan is the contractor of sin and we are the subcontractors performing his job for him. Through our weaknesses, Satan rents our souls to get his job of destruction accomplished. Did you notice I did not say construction? Satan does not construct anything. He destructs everything in his path. Granted, we are all sinners and have fallen short of the glory of God (Romans 3:23).

That is why God sent His Son, Jesus, into the world. Jesus came to free us from the destruction of this world. This destruction is the bondage Satan places in our lives, which keeps us in the will of the world and not in the will of God. This is where Jesus comes in. Jesus is like the building inspector. He comes into our lives to assure us we need to build our lives on the Word of God and not in the ways of the world.

Let us stop renting our souls to Satan and the world. Begin by repenting of your sins, asking Jesus to come into your heart and life, and build a stronger foundation by praying and reading His Word daily. Have a great day, and God bless!

Retread

The backslider in heart will be filled with his own ways,
But a good man *will be satisfied* from above.
The simple believes every word,
But the prudent considers well his steps.

—Prov. 14:14-15

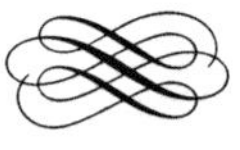

We begin life on this earth like a set of brand new tires. We start by rolling down life's unpredictable highway, not knowing what is around the next corner. We approach many traffic lights and stop signs in our life. Often, we are not sure which way to turn, and many times we turn the wrong way and end up at a dead end. We then turn around in order to go back to where we came from. We go back through the same old trials and sins we thought we left behind. Once we get past all the mess, we notice all that sin has worn down our tires. We slip into more trouble at every turn, because we do not have any traction because the road we are traveling on is wet and slick from the tears of our pain and hurts.

The future doesn't look any better, but it can. You can have either an "all-weather radial" tire or a "Goodlife." It is like an extended warranty for eternity. It is up to you.

How is this possible after all the roadblocks and dead ends you have run into? Well, first, you have to deflate yourself of your pride and go flat, releasing everything to Jesus. Then, ask Jesus to retread your soul, which is your tire, and pump you up with the Holy Spirit. Then He will spin and balance your life and will roll you off in the direction you need to be heading. The direction is down a one-way road leading to the cross. God bless!

Return to Sender

Where do wars and fights *come* from among you? Do *they* not *come* from your *desires for* pleasure that war in your members? You lust and do not have. You murder and covet and cannot obtain. You fight and war. Yet you do not have because you do not ask. You ask and do not receive, because you ask amiss, that you may spend *it* on your pleasures. Adulterers and adulteresses! Do you know that friendship with the world is enmity with God? Whoever therefore wants to be a friend of the world makes himself an enemy of God.

—James 4:1-4

Have you ever written a letter to a friend you had not heard from in years and sent it off in the mail, only to receive it back several days later, stamped: "Return to Sender. Address Unknown"? You verified the address and sent it off again. Once again, it came back.

That's kind of like our prayer life. We get so busy in our lives that we forget about the One who sent His Son, Jesus, to die on the cross for our sins. Our jobs, our hobbies, the hustle and bustle of life, and other worldly temptations consume us so that we forget where God pulled us from in the past. However, let something happen in our lives that knocks us for a loop, such as an illness, death, an unexpected pregnancy, or the loss of a job, and what is the first thing we do? We run to God. We pray about our circumstances. We pray, but nothing happens, so we pray again, but the same thing happens—nothing. It is like that letter you wrote to the friend you haven't spoken to in years. It came back to you, unanswered.

I don't know what you were expecting, since you forgot about your friend. You were so busy that you didn't even notice your friend had moved. That is kind of like our walk with God; however, we are the ones who move away from Him. God never moves away from us. He is always there.

Do you wonder why God does not answer your prayer when you run back to him? The reason is that you have been running away from God so long that you have collected much sin in your heart. God cannot work in your heart full of sin. The first thing you must do is ask God to forgive you of your sins. Especially, ask God to forgive you for walking away from Him and His will for your life. Then God can redeem you and begin working in your life again.

Don't get lost in the mail. Be delivered today and never return to your old ways. Send God a "knee-mail" on a daily basis. Always remember that neither rain, nor sleet, nor snow can stop God. No matter what type of storm you are going through, God will deliver you through it—not around it. Have a great day!

Reverse Interrogation

So it was that the beggar died, and was carried by the angels to Abraham's bosom. The rich man also died and was buried. And being in torments in Hades, he lifted his eyes and saw Abraham afar off, and Lazarus in his bosom.

Then he cried and said, 'Father Abraham, have mercy on me, and send Lazarus that he may dip the tip of his finger in water and cool my tongue; for I am tormented in this flame.' But Abraham said, 'Son, remember that in your lifetime you received your good things, and likewise Lazarus evil things; but now he is comforted and you are tormented. And besides all this, between us and you there is a great gulf fixed, so that those who want to pass from here to you cannot, nor can those from there pass to us.'

Then he said, 'I beg you therefore, father, that you would send him to my father's house, for I have five brothers, that he may testify to them, lest they also come to this place of torment.' Abraham said to him, 'They have Moses and the prophets; let them hear them.' And he said, 'No, father

> Abraham, but if one goes to them from the dead, they will repent.' But he said to him, 'If they do not hear Moses and the prophets, neither will they be persuaded though one rise from the dead.'
>
> —Luke 16:22-31

If you have ever watched a detective show on television, you have probably seen someone interrogated for a crime the cops accused him or her of committing. Usually, there are two detectives in the room with the suspect. There are also one or two detectives behind a two-way mirror, watching the process in order to make sure that they do everything by the book, which is the law.

Let us take a murder case and look at the some of the questions the interrogators might ask. They may ask the suspect some of the following questions: "Where were you on a particular night during the hours in question," "When was the last time you saw this person alive?" "What is your relationship to this person?," and, "Was he a friend or a coworker of yours?"

At this point, you may be wondering what the title "Reverse Interrogation" means. I am sure you heard of a normal interrogation before, but never a reverse interrogation. Consider the following scenario, and I will show you what I mean by it. Say you had a friend you have known all your life. You did everything together while growing up. You fished, rode bikes, and played Army together. The only time you were apart was when you went home to eat or went to bed for the night. Other than that, you two were inseparable. You were with each other all week long, at least six out of seven days of the week. The one day of the week you didn't see much of each other was Sunday. That was the day you would get up with your family and go to church to hear the gospel preached. Then one Sunday, on October 7, 2001, something happened that would change your life forever. Jesus saved you when you accepted Him as your Lord and personal Savior at the age of ten. You went home that Sunday afternoon and saw your friend, but you never told him what happened to you that day. As the years flew by, before you knew it, the two of you were graduating from high school, and after the summer break, you headed off to different colleges in different states. You had spent the summer together doing what teenagers do and then the summer ended. You said your goodbyes, went your separate ways, and began a new chapter in your lives. You headed to a Christian college to become a preacher and started a ministry. Your friend went to a different college, had good intentions, but didn't make it through the first semester. He dropped out of school and started hanging around the wrong crowd. One night it cost him his life. On October 7, many years later, the same day you were saved, your friend died.

You did not find out what happened to your friend until spring break, and it devastated you to hear the news. Then one night you have a dream. Your friend comes into your dream and begins to interrogate you for his murder. That is right, his murder! As far as he is concerned, you are the prime suspect in his case. He proceeds to ask you, "Where were you on the night of October 7, the night I died and went to hell? Why did you not tell me about Jesus, how He could save me, and how it would have changed my life forever if I had only accepted Him as my Savior? If it were not for you, friend, I wouldn't be here right now burning up. We were best friends our whole lives. Now, my life has ended and it is a living hell. Friends do not let friends die and go to hell! So, friend, this is the end. Goodbye forever."

Do not let this happen to you. Tell everyone you see, friend or foe, about Jesus. God bless, and have a great day!

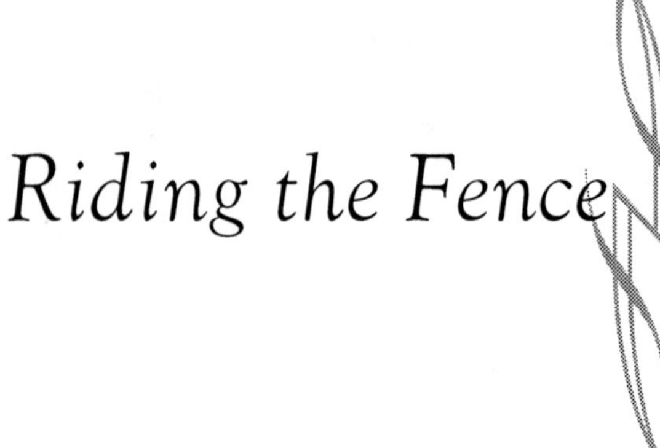

Riding the Fence

Therefore, my beloved, as you have always obeyed, not as in my presence only, but now much more in my absence, work out your own salvation with fear and trembling; for it is God who works in you both to will and do for *His* good pleasure.

Do all things without complaining and disputing, that you may become blameless and harmless, children of God without fault in the midst of a crooked and perverse generation, among whom you shine as lights in the world, holding fast the word of life, so that I may rejoice in the day of Christ that I have not run in vain or labored in vain.

—Phil. 2:12-16

I am sure most of you have heard of the singing group The Eagles. They wrote a song in 1973 called "Desperado." It is a song about a man out riding fences. He is alone on the range, riding along fences and repairing those damaged by livestock or man.

He is kind of like Jesus. Jesus is always repairing the fences in our Christian walk. We are always knocking down our fences or destroying them when we ride them like a cowboy, not knowing on which side of the fence we should be. Usually, we end up on the wrong side. Satan, the evil deceiver, constantly reminds us of something we used to do and liked to do in our past.

Sometimes, we choose to do those things again. He will tempt you continually with something from your past, to try to get you to break through your fence or ride it until it breaks, just to get you to follow him. He makes your past look so much easier than the present life you now have with Jesus. Your former way of life probably was easier because you had no one telling you what you should or shouldn't do. You see, when you do not have Jesus in your life, Satan doesn't care one thing about you because he still has you, and you both are heading in the same direction. Once you find Jesus, all hell breaks loose. This infuriates Satan when he loses one of his souls to Jesus Christ. See, he knows the power of a changed life. Satan knows we have victory through Jesus Christ, and he sends his demons from hell to try to pull you back down with him.

Once you have Jesus, however, you have Jesus for life. If you stick with the world, Satan's stomping ground, he will stomp you right into the grave and will deceive you into thinking you don't have a chance in hell of getting to heaven. Look to the cross, which is life, and repair your fences daily with the Word of God and through prayer. Have a great day!

River

"LORD, make me to know my end,
And what *is* the measure of my days,
That I may know how frail I *am*.
Indeed, You have made my days as handbreadths,
And my age *is* as nothing before You;
Certainly every man at his best
state *is* but vapor. **(Selah)**
Surely every man walks about like a shadow;
Surely they busy themselves in vain;
He heaps up *riches*,
And does not know who will gather them.

—Ps. 39:4-6

There are many mighty rivers in the world, which all have various uses. Rivers can generate electricity and transport goods and people. Men have tried to control these rivers for centuries, but the rivers always win. We try to change the course of these powerful rivers by building levees, dams, and locks.

What we need to do, however, is change the courses of our lives. If we compare our lives to a barge on the river, we can see how the two relate to each other. Let us compare our lives to a tugboat that pushes barges up the Mississippi River, one of the largest and most powerful rivers in the world. The tugboat has a tremendous amount of resistance pushing against its hull. This resistance creates a lot of stress and pressure on the barge's hull, just like the pressures we face on a daily basis.

Our lives would be so much better if we would learn to turn the boat (our life) around, go with the flow, and stop resisting God. I work along the Mississippi River and see the barges fighting this resistance on the river every day. From where I work, one can see two bridges that sit about one-half mile apart. We have timed these barges as they travel against the current. It takes about twenty minutes to travel from one bridge to the other. Pushing those barges up river wastes so much time, energy, and fuel. It would drive me crazy if I had to do that job for a living. However, if you think about it, we waste a lot of time and energy fighting and resisting against God's will for our lives. It is a fight we will never win.

If we would just surrender our lives to Jesus and let Him handle the pressures and stress we face daily, our lives would flow more smoothly. Have a great day, and do not push away from God. Flow into Him! God bless!

Road Trip

Let your eyes look straight ahead,
And your eyelids look right before you.
Ponder the path of your feet,
And let all your ways be established.
Do not turn to the right or left;
Remove your foot from evil.

—Prov. 4:25-27

The Christian walk is a lot like a road that goes on forever—at least it seems that way. Most road trips can be very enjoyable when the road is smooth and there are no hazards or detours. However, we know it is not always like that. Something always happens or gets in our way.

Have you ever planned a road trip and mapped it out so that nothing would go wrong? Then, it didn't turn out as you'd planned. Sound familiar? You start out on your road trip and everything is going fine. Then you hit rush hour traffic. I never understood why they call it "rush hour" when you're not even moving, and it takes longer than usual to get to your destination. Then you finally get moving, so you put the pedal to the metal to make up for lost time. You set your cruise control at 75 to 80 miles an hour. You are cruising down the road and then it happens: you see blue lights in your rearview mirror. If you're lucky, you get off with a warning. Then you get rolling again, and for the next one-hundred miles you make great time. Then once again, it happens: Satan comes into the picture. He throws a detour in your path, and you did not intend to get lost. You take the detour and it is full of temptations, setbacks, and sin! You try to be strong, but Satan is crafty. He knows what you like, what will draw you in and make you sin, and he makes your road very bumpy. You try to turn back, but the last storm washed the bridge away, so you travel down the road feeling bad for what you had done. However, there is hope down the road.

At some point, we all come to an intersection in our sinful drive. It is a four-way stop and it is there for a reason. It makes us stop and think about how much we need Jesus in our drive through life. If we turn right, there is sin and if we turn left, there is more sin. However, straight ahead, there is the valley of the sin we are already in. If we ask Jesus to guide us, He will get us through the valley and back on the road, which will lead to the mountaintop, to an elevation from where we can see the light.

Don't look into your rearview mirror at where you have been. Break it off and throw it out the window, so you won't be able to look back at where you were. Then, just gaze through the windshield and set your eyes on Jesus. God bless and God speed!

Rodeo

But the salvation of the righteous *is* from the LORD;
He is their strength in the time of trouble.
And the LORD shall help them and deliver them;
He shall deliver them from the wicked,
And save them,
Because they trust in Him.

—Ps. 37:39-40

Being conformed to the world is a lot like riding a Brahma bull at a rodeo. It has many ups and downs, a lot of spin, and a lot of kick in it. Everything is fine as long as you and the bull are contained in the shoot. As soon as that gate swings open, however, all hell breaks loose and you are at the mercy of the bull, which in this case is the world.

The world will take you for the ride of your life and may even take your life. Even though the ride might seem like an eternity, it lasts only eight seconds or less. Then it is over. It's kind of like when we sin. It doesn't take very long to commit the sin, but it seems to take us an eternity to pay for our sins and repent of them. We need to repent as soon as we commit the sin. Unfortunately, we are a lot like the bull. We kick, we spin, we buck and snort, we are up and down, and we are just plain bull-headed. We must grab life by the thorns and not by the horns in order to take our life to the next level. We need to herd up all the sin in our lives, and take it to the hills of Calvary and lay it at the foot of the cross to let the One who died for our sins cover it with the blood He shed.

Jesus Christ was the One who died and shed His blood on that cross for your sins and mine. He is willing to round up your sin and take it out of your life forever. So, don't get caught in the reigns of the world and get bullied around. Come under the reigns of Jesus Christ; the One who reigns forever. Have a great day, and God bless!

Rumor Seeds

Where *there is* no wood, the fire goes out;
And where *there is* no talebearer, strife ceases.
As charcoal *is* to burning coals, and wood to fire,
So *is* a contentious man to kindle strife.
The words of a talebearer *are* like tasty trifles,
And they go down into the inmost body.
He who hates, disguises *it* with his lips,
And lays up deceit within himself;
When he speaks kindly, do not believe him,
For *there are* seven abominations in his heart;
A lying tongue hates *those who are* crushed by it,
And a flattering mouth works ruins.

—Prov. 26:20-25, 28

Everyone, Christian or not, can be classified as a seed that either produces life or destroys it. A seed that produces life is one that produces much fruit when sown in the right environment. The sun and water nurture it until it is ready for harvesting. A seed that destroys life, such as a rumor, is harmless. However, once stirred up, picked up by the wind, and spread over the land like a plague infesting the fields of life. It starts out as a tiny seed lying on the ground, rocks, or road. Many seeds will find themselves stepped on, trampled under foot, and destroyed. However, sun will scorch and burn up the seeds lying in the fields, which is the church, if left on top of the ground. If a conflict arises in the church, the dirt begins flying around. With all this dirt flying around, the dirt covers the seeds. Once the dirt settles, every thing seems to be fine—but it's not. The soil within the church covers the seed.

When a seed starts to germinate and take root, it begins as a harmless vine—or looks harmless. Then it touches someone who is weak and hurting. The vine is like poison ivy. As soon as it touches you, you get the itch to tell someone something, not based on facts or isn't true. Then that person gets the itch to tell someone else, and so on and so on. The vine becomes so strong that it can choke the life out of the church.

Let us stop the rumors. If we get the itch to start or spread a rumor, let's medicate ourselves with the Word of God, the most powerful medicine there is. Stay medicated in the Word so the rash won't spread. Have a great day and stay out of the woods!

Scanners

The law of the LORD *is* perfect, converting the soul;
The testimony of the LORD *is* sure, making wise the simple;
The statutes of the LORD *are* right, rejoicing the heart;
The commandment of the LORD *is* pure, enlightening the eyes;
The fear of the LORD *is* clean, enduring forever;
The judgments of the LORD *are* true *and* righteous altogether.
More to be desired *are they* than gold,
Yea, than much fine gold;
Sweeter also than honey and the honeycomb.
Moreover by them Your servant is warned,
And in keeping them *there is* great reward.
Who can understand *his* errors?
Cleanse me from secret *faults*.
Keep back Your servant also from presumptuous *sins*;
Let them not have dominion over me.
Then I shall be blameless,

And I shall be innocent of great transgression.
Let the words of my mouth and the meditation of my heart
Be acceptable in Your sight,
O LORD, my strength and my Redeemer.

—Ps. 19: 7-14

Have you ever wondered if our sins are tracked or stored? Well I have come up with an off-the-wall idea. When we are born, we would have a bar code implanted in our hearts and every time we sinned, a scanner that revolved around the earth every 24 hours would pick it up. It would pick up unconfessed sins we had in our hearts. If we repented of our sins within a 24-hour period, however, God would forgive us of that sin and the scanner would not pick it up. If we didn't repent within that 24-hour period, the scanner would come around and scan the sin remaining in our hearts and record them. If the scanner calculated your sin every 24 hours, every day of your life until you died, can you imagine how much sin that would add up to if you never repented?

It is phenomenal, if you think about it, because I did not get saved and repent of my sins until I was 40 years old. Forty years! That is a lot of sin! If I had a bar code, I probably would have worn it out. Most likely, it wouldn't scan anymore.

Imagine if you sinned once a day for 40 years and multiplied that by 365 days. That equals 14,600 sins committed over a 40-year period. That is very scary if you think about it. For most of us, that number is probably even higher. If you are a Christian, however, you know this isn't the way it works. When you asked Jesus to come into your life and you repented of your sins, God forgave you. He erased your sins and will no longer bring them up again.

Think of how much sin was dumped on Jesus as He hung on the cross on Calvary—all the sins from the past, present, and future. I thought my sins were too much, but just think—Jesus took away the sins of the world. It blows my mind just to think of how high the number would be if God counted all of our sins. If you don't know Jesus as your personal Lord and Savior, all you have to do is ask Him to come live inside your heart and life, and repent of your sins. You must mean it with every fiber of your being. He will forgive you of all your sins and He will change your life forever. Selah! Think about it!

Seaworthy or Unworthy

Depart! Depart! Go out from there,
Touch no unclean *thing*;
Go out from the midst of her,
Be clean,
You who bear the vessels of the Lord.
For you shall not go out with haste,
Nor go by flight;
For the LORD will go before you,
And the God of Israel *will be* your rear guard.

—Isa. 52:11-12

Before becoming a Christian, we could compare our lives to a ship lost at sea. The reason it is lost is that it has no captain; therefore, there is no guidance, discipline, or leadership. It is just a vessel full of lost souls relying on their own judgment and guidance.

Where does it get you when you rely on the lost leading the lost? More lost! You are out there drifting from port to starboard, never sailing on an even keel. You find yourself sailing into storms. Every time a storm ends, you come out more battered and more lost. Your ship has gone astray at sea for so long that many barnacles begin to weigh it down, which are like unforgiven sin in your life. The worm that lives inside the barnacles begins to eat the wood of your life, which is your ship. Holes start to penetrate your hull, and you begin to take on water, which weighs you down even more. Then you begin to sink. You sink so much that you have no control of the ship, which is your life. Because of the excess weight of your sin, the rudder snaps off in your last sinful endeavor. You drift aimlessly for what seems like an eternity. You finally run aground, into a sandbar. As you sit on the sandbar, you try to think of a way to free yourself from this predicament, but you sit there for days trying to think of a way out.

The only way to free yourself is to surrender and ask Jesus Christ to come into your life. Jesus can pull you from your sin, clean you up, scrape the barnacles (sin) from your hull, and patch the holes in your life. The scraping might be painful. However, nothing compares to the pain Jesus suffered on the cross for our sins. Let Jesus set a new direction in your life. Allow Him to control the rudder so that your life can stay on an even keel and sail into eternity with Him as your captain. Have a great day and don't let your life be a Titanic!

Shifting Tides

There is therefore now no condemnation to those who are in Christ Jesus, who do not walk according to the flesh, but according to the Spirit. For the law of the Spirit of life in Christ Jesus has made me free from the law of sin and death. For what the law could not do in that it was weak through the flesh, God *did* by sending His own Son in the likeness of sinful flesh, on account of sin: He condemned sin in the flesh, that the righteous requirement of the law might be fulfilled in us who do not walk according to the flesh but according to the Spirit. For those who live according to the flesh set their minds on the things of the flesh, but those *who live* according to the Spirit, the things of the Spirit. For to be carnally minded *is* death, but to be spiritually minded *is* life and peace. Because the carnal mind *is* enmity against God; for it is not subject to the law of God, nor indeed can be. So then, those who are in the flesh cannot please God.

But you are not in the flesh but in the Spirit, if indeed the Spirit of God dwells in you. Now if anyone does not have

> the Spirit of Christ, he is not His. And if Christ *is* in you, the body *is* dead because of sin, but the Spirit *is* life because of righteousness. But if the Spirit of Him who raised Jesus from the dead dwells in you, He who raised Christ from the dead will also give life to your mortal bodies through His Spirit who dwells in you.
>
> —Rom. 8:1-11

I am sure many of us have been to the beach at some point in our lives and have noticed the footprints we left behind in the sand as we walked along the edge of the beach. This is sometimes like our Christian walk. For some, it is all the time. We often walk on the edge to see how close we can get to sin before we fall into it. With our sinful nature, however, standing near the edge of sin is too close for us, because often we cannot control the flesh. If we get too close to sin, we will fall in. Our flesh is so weak that we need someone to remind us continually and stop us before we get too close to sin.

That is were the Holy Spirit comes in. We need to work with the Holy Spirit to allow Him to work within us and through us in our lives. Most of the time, we don't listen to our hearts, where the Holy Spirit resides. Often, we think with our mind, which is such a dangerous thing to do, because our mind has become so corrupt from the world we live in. We fill our mind with all the junk we see in our daily walk on this earth. Often, we allow our minds to take control of our walk instead of our hearts. We need to shift things around and begin thinking with our hearts first and then apply that to our mind. It is not an easy shift to make when you live in this world; however, it's what we have to do if we want to live a victorious Christian life in such a corrupt world.

We must pay attention to the tide, which in this case would be the tide of sin. We must walk in alertness, paying close attention to the shifting tides, high and low. We need to walk our Christian walk as if it is always at high tide; that way, when the tides do change, we will be less likely to sin. However, when the tide goes out, which is low tide, most of us venture too far out. We get comfortable at low tide and sometimes forget where we are. When the tide shifts again, by the time we notice that it has changed, it is too late to get back to where we once were. Then it happens: the rip tide of sin catches and carries us so far out that we know we can't get back under our own strength. We think we will never get back to where we once were in our fellowship with God at high tide.

That is the problem—we think too much with our minds and not our hearts. We must shift our thinking from our minds to our hearts. Ask Jesus to come pull you from the current of sin and have Him place you back at high tide and back into fellowship with God. Stay on the beach. Stay at high tide and be aware of what is in front of you. Have a blessed day!

Shopping Carts

Therefore let us pursue the things *which make* for peace and the things by which one may edify another. Do not destroy the work of God for the sake of food. All things indeed *are* pure, but *it is* evil for the man who eats with offense. *It is* good neither to eat meat nor drink wine nor *do anything* by which your brother stumbles or is offended or is made weak. Do you have faith? Have *it* to yourself before God. Happy *is* he who does not condemn himself in what he approves. But he who doubts is condemned if he eats, because *he does* not *eat* from faith; for whatever *is* not from faith is sin.

—Rom. 14:19-23

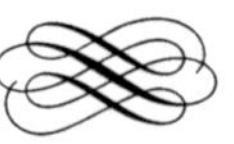

When you are a Christian, you must be in a constant state of awareness because somebody is always watching you and waiting for you to mess up. The person watching you might be a fellow Christian. You wouldn't think it would be like that, but a fellow Christian is often your worst enemy. You would expect this kind of behavior from a non-Christian. The ones who watch you the most are those who cost you the most.

For example, you go to the grocery store to do your shopping. There people are watching what you put into your shopping cart to buy. They know you proclaim to be a Christian. Will you be able to prove to them that you're not the same person by not buying the things you used to buy? What happens when you leave town and go on vacation? Are the items in your shopping cart still going to reflect who and what you profess to be? Think about it. You are hundreds of miles from home. There is nobody around who knows anything about you or who you are. Are you going to fail or prevail?

I think a lot of us would fail in this situation because the temptations of this world increase when you are alone and not around family and fellow Christians. I'm not saying everyone would fail, but some of us would. Even though you may be hundreds of miles from home, it doesn't mean you are not going to bump shopping carts with someone you know. I have been overseas in a third-world country and have run into people I knew. I was shocked to see them in such a faraway country. I had nothing to hide back then because God hadn't saved me yet, so there was no harm done. At least, I thought that way back then.

Don't ever get comfortable where you are shopping. Always shop as if someone is watching you. Remember, if the world isn't watching, God is! Don't get caught with things you shouldn't have bought, but be bought by the One who purchased you with His blood, Jesus Christ. Have a great day, and God bless!

Short Circuit

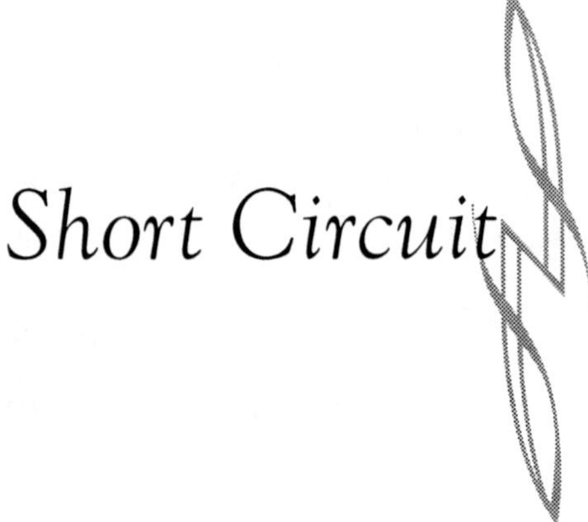

But we have this treasure in earthen vessels, that the excellence of the power may be of God and not of us. *We are* hard-pressed on every side, yet not crushed; *we are* perplexed, but not in despair; persecuted, but not forsaken; struck down, but not destroyed—always carrying about in the body the dying of the Lord Jesus, that the life of Jesus also may be manifested in our body.

—2 Cor. 4:7-10

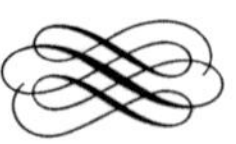

Christians have many positive and negative things happen to us every day. Unfortunately, there are more negative than positive things. Most of the time, we bring on the negative stuff ourselves. If we would only put God first in our lives, we would still experience the negative in our lives, but we would have peace and joy in the midst of it all. We don't always put

God first, so we kind of short-circuit ourselves from God's blessings in our lives.

Let us look at ourselves as if we were a circuit, such as a plug. You have three wires, which make a circuit. There are a positive wire, a negative wire, and a ground wire. If you look at the positive wire, which supplies the power, this represents the power of God. The negative wire represents us, and the ground wire is where we should be—grounded in the Word of God. However, our sinful nature always wants to disconnect us from God's positive power. Our lives become negative, depressing and without meaning, when we unplug ourselves from our "power source".

Let us stay fully connected and let God supply the power to our lives. I consider my life sometimes like a circuit breaker. I may trip, but Jesus is always there to reset me and give me the power and strength for the next power surge. Have a great day and stay grounded!

Shortcuts

But, beloved, do not forget this one thing, that with the Lord one day *is* as a thousand years, and a thousand years as one day. The Lord is not slack concerning *His* promise, as some count slackness, but is longsuffering toward us, not willing that any should perish but that all should come to repentance.

—2 Peter 3:8-9

When we conform to this world, or even when we proclaim to be a Christian, we are always trying to find shortcuts to get the job done faster. However, we all know that faster isn't always better. Often, shortcuts cause more problems than they are worth. If we always took shortcuts, we would never know the true fulfillment of completing a challenging project, and we would never go into a challenge with our whole heart.

Just think what would have happened if God had taken shortcuts when He came into this world in the form of a baby, our Savior, Jesus Christ. What if God had bypassed the virgin birth? Would we still have hope? Would we still have followed *Jesus* or would we have seen Him as just another man with great wisdom? What if Jesus had taken a shortcut? What if He never went to the cross? Would we still have the hope of salvation? I think not.

Thank God, our God is nothing like us. We must be more like Him. We need to praise God every second of the day that He is not a shortcut God but that He went all the way and put His whole heart into seeing there was a way for our salvation. That way is through His Son, Jesus, who provided a way when there was no way on the cross at Calvary. Stop taking shortcuts and go the distance. Tell everyone you meet about how Jesus Christ can save him or her. God bless, and have a great day!

Solo Act

Thus says the Lord:
"Cursed *is* the man who trusts in man
And makes flesh his strength,
Whose heart departs from the Lord.
For he shall be like a shrub in the desert,
And shall not see when good comes,
But shall inhabit the parched
 places in the wilderness,
In a salt land *which is* not inhabited.

—Jer. 17:5-6

When Jesus saves us, we are supposed to rely fully on God. However, there are many times we do not rely on God or trust Him, as we should with everything we have. We are to seek God's approval in everything we do, but we like doing things our own way. When we do things our way, they rarely work out the way we planned. The words "me" and "I" are solo words. They need to be "us," which means "together." "I" need to work together with God and not apart from Him, for with God, all things are possible (Mark 10:27). "I" am just one part of the whole.

Unfortunately, I am the one part that is full of pride. I try to be a solo act, trying to accomplish things, which I want but God does not. If only I would surrender my pride and not allow it to hold me back my life would be so much better. Pride prevents me from releasing everything, including my past, to God. Unfortunately, flying solo is a whole lot easier than trying to work as a team. That is why I tend to lean more toward being solo. I have nobody telling me what to do and nobody checking up on me or holding me accountable. The one, big problem of being solo, however, is I am alone. And not if, but when, I fall I will fall hard, and there will be nobody to catch me or pick me up. Often, while I am down I may end up getting even farther away from God. The whole time I am away from God, the farther away I get from Christian fellowship. Christian fellowship is a big part of our walk. Unless you like talking to yourself, it is difficult to fellowship when you are flying solo.

We must be more like Jesus and follow His example. Jesus did His Father's will and not His own. Jesus fulfilled everything His Father had planned for Him. When Jesus was in the Garden of Gethsemane, He cried out to His Father: "Father if it is Your will, take this cup away from Me. Nevertheless, not My will but Your will be done" (Luke 22:42). Jesus did His Father's will. He went all the way to Calvary to die on the cross for our sins and the sins of the world.

You see, God Himself has a team. It is a three-in-one operation, which is God, Jesus, and the Holy Spirit. They work together to accomplish anything and everything. Don't be a solo act because, before you know it, you'll be so low in your life and so deep in the darkness that you won't be able to see your faults and failures. Look up and come out of the darkness and into the light, where you can see the error of your ways. Once you see them, hand them over to Jesus. Become a team player and start sharing in the victory Jesus has already provided for us. All we have to do is claim the victory! We win!

Soul Repair

Answer me speedily, O LORD;
My spirit fails!
Do not hide Your face from me,
Lest I be like those who go down into the pit.
Cause me to hear Your lovingkindness in the morning,
For in You do I trust;
Cause me to know the way in which I should walk,
For I lift up my soul to You.

—Ps. 143:7-8

The Christian walk is often like a good pair of shoes. The shoes look and feel good. When they look good, you feel good, so your walk looks good. When our walk is good, however, we sometimes get so confident that pride can set in. Then it happens: someone steps on you and your shoes, which were once shiny, become dull, scratched, and dirty.

Our whole attitude changes when this happens. Our once-confident walk becomes a limp or a shuffle. We begin dragging our feet and, eventually, the "soul" of our shoes begins to wear out. We start getting holes in our souls, and our feet get wet. Then, dirt invades our souls, and they become infected so badly that we feel like a heel.

The way to repair your soul is to seek the "Soul Healer," which can be found only in the Lord Jesus Christ. He is the only One who can repair the holes in our souls and put back the shine in our lives. So kick up your heels and go be a soul winner for Jesus.

Standby

But of that day and hour no one knows, not even the angels of heaven, but My Father only. But as the days of Noah *were*, so also will be the coming of the Son of Man be. For as in the days before the flood, they were eating and drinking, marrying and giving in marriage, until the day that Noah entered the ark, and did not know until the flood came and took them all away, so also will be the coming of the Son of Man be. Then two *men* will be in the field: one will be taken and the other left. Two *women will be* grinding at the mill: one will be taken and the other left. Watch therefore, for you do not know what hour your Lord is coming. But know this, that if the master of the house had known what hour the thief would come, he would have watched and not allowed his house to be broken into. Therefore you also be ready, for the Son of Man is coming at an hour you do not expect.

—Matt. 24:36-44

If you have served in the military, you have heard of the word "standby." It means that you must be ready at a moment's notice. You must be available for immediate action to fight a war in your own country or in a foreign land to set someone free. As I write this, there are men and women on standby to fight a war for someone's freedom in Iraq and Afghanistan. The men and woman I am talking about live in our neighborhoods and go to our churches. They are leaving knowing there is a chance they might not come back home alive and in one piece! I do not know how many will die, but we Christians need to tell them how they can live even when they may die. As Christians, we need to stop standing by, watching and knowing they might be going to hell when they die, with no chance of life after they depart from this world.

Let us stop standing by. Instead, let us start standing up and stepping out to tell people how they can have eternal life with Jesus Christ. Stand up for what you believe and tell everyone you see about Jesus and how He stood up for what He believed as He hung on the cross and died for our sins. Tell them how, three days later, He stood up and stepped out of the grave—and in doing so, defeated death, hell, and the grave. Do you know what the greatest news is? He did this all for us. God bless, and have a great life!

Static Cling

I will behave wisely in a perfect way.
Oh, when will You come to me?
I will walk within my house with a perfect heart.
I will set nothing wicked before my eyes;
I hate the work of those who fall away;
It shall not cling to me.
A perverse heart shall depart from me;
I will not know wickedness.

—Ps. 101:2-4

When most men wash their dirty laundry, they throw everything in together. They don't separate the darks from the lights, they wash the laundry at the wrong temperature, or they add too much detergent. Sound familiar? When it comes time to put the stuff in the dryer, well, that is a different story in itself. It drives my wife crazy when I put my stuff in the dryer and I don't use a dryer sheet in the load. Everything comes out stuck together with static cling. I thought the purpose of static cling was so that your socks would stick to your clothes so you wouldn't lose them. I hate losing one sock. You throw away the one you have, and then a week later you find the other one inside your pant leg.

Let us compare our Christian walk to the static we find in our dryers. We try to live a good Christian life. However, with all the stresses we deal with on a daily basis, we build up a lot of static. This causes us to fall back into our sinful nature, and once we let our guard down, it is hard to get our guard back up. The static we have in our lives begins attracting sin. Then the sin sticks to us as the sock stuck to our pants. We try to shake the sin from our lives, but it just keeps coming back. When the sin comes back, it brings more sin and more static with it; and the more we try to shake it off, the more static we create. Now, we are in worse shape and deeper in our sin than before.

Being a Christian is a constant battle of trying to stay clean. We know we cannot do this on our own. We need to ask Jesus to take away our sin as only He can. When Jesus died on the cross on Calvary for our sins, the blood He shed covered us and washed away our sins. It is kind of the same principle with the static and sin we still have in our lives.

Let Jesus come in and run us through the wash cycle, and let Him dry us in the dryer, which represents the fire of purification. He will then cover us with His blood, which in the dryer, is like a dryer sheet. This, in turn, would remove the static and sin we have in our lives. Remember Jesus when you start to feel the static building up in your life. Let Him take it away. Let us cling to Jesus. He is the one who can free us of any static we may encounter in our lives. Have a blessed day!

Strings

"I taught Ephraim to walk,
Taking them by their arms;
But they did not know that I healed them.
I drew them with gentle cords
With bands of love,
And I was to them as those who take the yoke from their neck.
I stooped *and* fed them."

—Hos. 11:3-4

Have you ever felt as if someone has tied you down or is controlling you by strings? Many strings attach you to this world. There is your job, your friends and family, and your addictions. It's like a power controls you but you can't see, hear, or feel it. It's as if you are a puppet on a string, putting on a show for the world to see.

Most of you have heard the story of Pinocchio, the puppet that wanted to become a real boy. Like us, he also had strings attached and someone controlling him. The evil ruler and puppeteer of this world, Satan, controls us if we allow him to. Pinocchio's greatest downfall was his lying, and every time he would tell a lie, his nose would grow and grow. The only way it could return to normal was if he told the truth.

Imagine if we were like Pinocchio and all our sins were just like Pinocchio's lies. How long would your nose be? Can you imagine, noses poking into everyone's business, where he or she doesn't belong. What if the only way we could get our noses back to normal were to confess our sins and ask Jesus to forgive us, to come into our lives, change us, and make us new again? Jesus would then cut the strings that bind us to this world. The Holy Spirit will come to reside in our hearts and there will no longer be any strings attached to us to trip us up. Have a great day!

Super-Bouncy Ball

But in a great house there are not only vessels of gold and silver, but also of wood and clay, some for honor and some for dishonor. Therefore, if anyone cleanses himself from the latter, he will be a vessel for honor, sanctified and useful for the Master, prepared for every good work. Flee also youthful lusts; but pursue righteousness, faith, love, peace with those who call on the Lord out of a pure heart. But avoid foolish and ignorant disputes, knowing that they generate strife. And a servant of the Lord must not quarrel but be gentle to all, able to teach, patient, in humility correcting those who are in opposition, if God perhaps will grant them repentance, so that they may know the truth, and *that* they may come to their senses *and escape* the snare of the devil, having been taken captive by him to *do* his will.

—2 Tim. 2:20-26

Have you ever bought a super-bouncy ball out of a vending machine? Did you throw it at the ground as hard as you could to see how high it would bounce, and then try to keep track of where it went—only to lose sight of it? Once it hits the ground, it rebounds again and back down again and then ricochets off everything in its vicinity.

You can compare the action of this kind of ball to the actions we take in our Christian walk. In our walk, we often have many ups and downs, just like the ball. We all have different actions and reactions. At one moment, we are on the mountaintop and the next moment we are in the valley. Then we are back on the mountaintop and then back in the valley again. We bounce up and down and from side to side until; finally, we come to a resting point in the valley.

We shouldn't have to live like this, but most of us do. We are up and down constantly and in and out of our sins, and are being bounced constantly in many different directions by the world so often that we bounce back into our sins and into our old ways. The world builds up our confidence and bounces us around, which seems fine at the time, and then makes promises it doesn't keep. The world bounces us up the ladder of success and then drops us to see how high we bounce and where we end up.

Christians need to let God take control of our lives and these situations so we can stop bouncing back and forth in the world. We must focus on and look to the One who came to set us free from this world. Jesus came as a bouncing baby boy who grew into a man to whom sin could not attach itself. Sin bounced off Him and bounced back in Satan's face. Christians need to bounce back into fellowship with Jesus, stop letting the world tempt them, and let Jesus handle their life's ups and downs. Have a great day, and God bless!

The **D** Factor

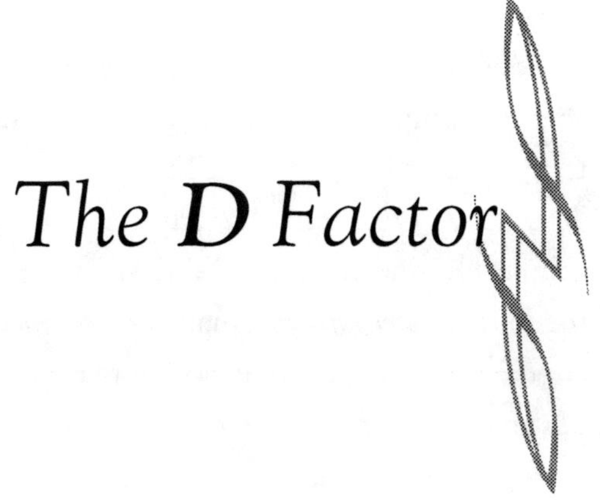

"Now therefore, listen to me, *my* children,
For blessed *are those who* keep my ways.
Hear instruction and be wise,
And do not distain it.
Blessed is the man who listens to me,
Watching daily at my gates,
Waiting at the posts of my doors.
For whoever finds me finds life,
And obtains favor from the LORD;
But he who sins against me wrongs his own soul;
All those who hate me love death."

—Prov. 8:32-36

I shared my testimony with some young men at my church. I explained to them what I had done in the past and that Jesus had forgiven me for what I had done. I prayed with them not to let the evil one get a hold of them and force them to travel the same path I had taken.

Before I spoke with them, I asked God how I could help them accomplish this and live a pure Christian life. God spoke to me almost in an instant. The letter *D* popped into my mind. The words Decisions, Determine, and Destination came into mind. The more I thought about them, the more sense they made. The *decisions* you make *determine* your *destination* if you choose not to accept Jesus as your personal Lord and Savior. Your destination isn't going to be very bright, and it will be very hot. However, if you choose to accept Jesus as your Lord and Savior your destination will be very bright.

Another thing God showed me was what many teens are involved in Drinking, Drugs, and Disobedience. The world is full of so many temptations which are so easy to get hold of and so readily available. Adults must step up and mentor these teenagers to prevent them from getting involved in drinking or drugs. These teenagers need to do three other things to live a pure Christian life. They need to be Different, Die to self and sin, and be Delivered from death to life through Jesus Christ, who gave His all on the cross at Calvary. This also applies to adults and young children. I pray one day that all these young men can stand up with a testimony saying, "I didn't do drugs, I didn't drink alcohol, I trusted Jesus through it all, and I am a better man today because of it!" Now that is a powerful testimony!

Have a great day, and may God deliver you and determine your destination!

The Net

But my eyes *are* upon You, O GOD the Lord;
In You I take refuge;
Do not leave my soul destitute.
Keep me from the snares they have laid for me,
And from the traps of the workers of iniquity.
Let the wicked fall into their own nets,
While I escape safely.

—Ps. 141:8-10

Most people these days either have a computer or have access to one at work or through a friend or family member. The computer is one of the greatest inventions ever made. We use it in so many ways for both good and evil. Many use the computer for good things, such as receiving e-mail, looking up useful things on the Internet, and helping us physically and spiritually. Unfortunately, where there is good, there is always evil lurking with every click of the mouse. Viruses can eat away at the files and hard drive and steal all your personal information stored on your computer. Hackers, who develop these viruses, are downright evil people. They can steal your information and, in turn, steal your identity for their own gain.

The word "hackers" stands for Hell's Attackers Causing the Kingpin of Evil to Rule your Soul. It is interesting to note that the word "inter" means to bury and "bury" means to conceal or hide or to become engrossed in. Using a sanctified imagination, I would define the word "Internet" to mean to be buried, or to hide or conceal, in a net. The Internet has stuff on the screen that lures you in like a fish to a hook. It uses bait, in the form of pop-up windows, to keep you coming back. Every time you come back for a nibble, the hook digs deeper and the harder it is to come back to reality, because the deeper you go the more entangled you become in the net. If you are not careful, you will no longer recognize the danger or warning signs anymore if you allow what you are looking at and doing to entice you.

All of a sudden, it happens! The net that entangles your mind ensnares you. Then you lose control, so you couldn't quit even if you wanted to. Once your mind has becomes entangled in the world, you become ensnared by the ways of the world.

Satan wants to keep you trapped in the net so he can control you and fill your mind with garbage. He wants to keep you submerged and he wants to take your breath away and drown your mind with lies. How can I avoid this from happening to me? You will need a firewall to protect you from the fiery darts Satan aims at you. Then you need to set up a virus scan to protect you from the evil one trying to steal your identity. You will need to track the attack to its origin and delete it from your life.

You will also need the support of a friend who will hold you accountable. But, most and foremost, you need to download the truth into your heart and life.

We find the truth in Jesus Christ. He is the way, the truth, and the life (John 14:6). He can keep you from diving into deep waters and getting caught in the net that leads to death and destruction. Don't believe any fish stories, because the more they are told, the bigger they get; and the bigger the fish, the more they stink. Have a great day!

The Price Is Right

For he who is called in the Lord *while* a slave is the Lord's freedman. Likewise he who is called *while* free is Christ's slave. You were bought at a price; do not become slaves of men. Brethren, let each one remain with God in that *state* in which he was called.

—1 Cor. 7:22-24

Have you ever seen the television show *The Price is Right*? If you haven't, I don't know where you have been the last fifty years! Those who are familiar with it know the show's contestants guess the prices of various items, which are there to bid on. Whoever comes closest without going over wins that item. That individual then gets to play a different game to try to win a bigger prize. Later in the show, that individual spins a big wheel. Whoever gets closest to one-dollar wins and gets a chance at a showcase of prizes.

Your life is the same way. We go though life with a price on our heads, and people are always trying to guess what it is and what it will take for us to follow them. However, in God's eyes, every life is priceless. God proved this when He left heaven and came to earth in human form as a baby named Jesus, to be born of a virgin and live among us for thirty-three years. Jesus did His Father's will, which was to die for our sins on the cross at Calvary. He defeated death, hell, and the grave.

Don't go through life trying to guess what it cost Jesus to die on the cross. It is priceless. You can't guess the price of what Jesus did for you and me, because it cost Him His life, and it cost God His one and only Son. Just remember the price was right, and we always win with Jesus. Sorry, Bob!

The Shadow of the Cross

For you were once darkness, but now *you are* light in the Lord. Walk as children of the light (for the fruit of the Spirit *is* in all goodness, righteousness, and truth), finding out what is acceptable to the Lord. And have no fellowship with the unfruitful works of darkness, but rather expose *them.* For it is shameful even to speak of those things which are done by them in secret. But all things that are exposed are made manifest by the light, for whatever makes manifest is light. Therefore He says:

"Awake, you who sleep,
Arise from the dead,
And Christ will give you light."

—Eph. 5:8-14

Most of those who say that Jesus saved them are running from the cross instead of to it. Often, when something negative happens in our lives, we run from it. For example, when a rumor gets started in your fellowship about someone you admired and placed your trust in, you leave to find another church. Unfortunately, this happens quite often. This just goes to show that we are putting our trust in man instead of in Jesus Christ. Instead of standing behind the cross, where we should be, we stand in front of the cross in its shadows. What we are saying is we don't need the light to see.

Eventually, some of us are going to stumble and fall into a pit so deep and dark that we won't be able to find our way out of the pit. It is so dark that it is hard to tell which way is up. Finally, we collapse and fall to our knees, crying out to Jesus to pull us from our pitiful life and have Him lead us back to the cross. The light there is so pure and bright. We are blinded by His brilliance—and should be because, being blinded, we must put our full trust in Jesus to guide us.

Let us walk by faith and not by sight (2 Corinthians 5:7) and trust Jesus to handle all our problems. There are no problems too big for Him to handle. Have a blessed day!

The Three Ps: Pride, Power, and Passion

The fear of the LORD *is* to hate evil;
Pride and arrogance and the evil way
And the perverse mouth I hate.

—Prov. 8:13

The reason many people do not surrender their lives to Jesus is pride. Pride stands for People Running Into Devil's Eternity. We must stop allowing the world to control our lives with worldly temptations and lies. If we could get past ourselves, lay down our pride, drop to our knees, ask God to forgive us of our sins, ask Jesus to come to live in our heart and let Him take control, we would be much better off. Satan, however, wants you to hold onto your pride, because once you surrender, he can't have you back and he hates that. Let us drop our pride and move on to a better life.

Once we surrender our pride, we can begin to see the power of God working in our lives. The word "Power" stands for People Overcoming the World's Evil Ruler. You would think with all the grace and goodness God has shown to us, we would never return to our old ways. Unfortunately, it goes to our head when God gives us the power. We think we can handle it in our own strength. We forget where God has brought us. The moment things begin to fall apart, we must realize our power isn't what will get us through the situation—it will be God. We must remember that we can do all things through Christ Jesus who strengthens us (Philippians 4:13). We are nothing without Him.

The final P is "Passion." Passion stands for Providing A Sacrifice and Suffering In Our Name. What a great word it is. Passion is what God showed us when He sent His Son, Jesus, to earth to live among us for thirty-three years. Passion is how Jesus showed us we should live and that we should love one another. However, the greatest passion of all is the passion Jesus showed us on the cross at Calvary, where He suffered and died for the sins of the world. All we have to do to receive it is repent of our sins and ask Jesus to come into our lives, change us, and make us new again. It is a free gift. It didn't cost us a dime, but it cost Jesus His life.

We know by the power and passion of our God that on the third day Jesus got up and walked out of the grave. He defeated death, hell, and the grave. He promised that He would return and take us home. One day God, His Father, will say, "Son, go get your children!" I can't wait for that day to come. Can you?

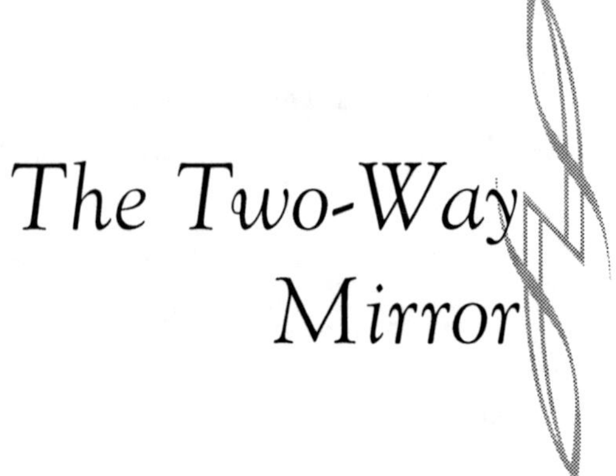

The Two-Way Mirror

Therefore lay aside all filthiness and overflow of wickedness, and receive with meekness the implanted word, which is able to save your souls.

But be doers of the word, and not hearers only, deceiving yourselves. For if anyone is a hearer of the word and not a doer, he is like a man observing his natural face in a mirror; for he observes himself, goes away and immediately forgets what kind of man he was. But he who looks into the perfect law of liberty and continues *in it*, and is not a forgetful hearer but a doer of the work, this one will be blessed in what he does.

—James 1:21-25

When you look into a mirror, do you like what you see? Many of us do not. They say that beauty is only skin deep, but some of us just have more skin than others have. We have often heard in church "God is good, all the time. God is good," but can you say that when you stand in front of the mirror? When you look at yourself, can you say, "Thank you, Jesus, for this body? You are so good to me."

Now, let us look at this from a different perspective. Let's say you look into your mirror, which is a two-way mirror. You are on one side of the mirror and God is on the other side. You might like what you see, but will God like what He sees? If we proclaim to be Christians, we are all supposed to reflect Jesus. Often, however, our reflections mirror more of what we are than what Jesus is in our lives. We need to switch sides with God and look at ourselves as God sees us, in hopes it will change the way we live if we see the reflection God sees of us and the reflection we cast for the world to see.

We all need to do better and we need to reflect back to what took place over 2,000 years ago. Jesus came to earth to be born of a virgin and lived a sinless life among His people for thirty-three years. He showed them how to reflect their love to one another and how they should live their lives. He reflected His love when He went all the way to Calvary for our sins and the sins of the world. Then He rose from the grave and went to be with His Father in heaven. He sent a reflection of Himself once again to comfort us and keep us holy, and He lives in our hearts. He is the Holy Spirit. Often we crowd out the Holy Spirit with our own selfishness. We reflect more of ourselves, which is the flesh, from our hearts than we reflect the Spirit.

We must look in the mirror every morning to make sure that what we see is what God wants us to be. Unfortunately, our mirror becomes so clouded with unrepented sins that what we see is not what we are supposed to be. Let us repent of our sins so we can get a true reflection of who we are now and who God want us to be in the future. It is important to dig into the Word of God daily to renew the Spirit within us.

Have a great day, and reflect God's love to someone today. God bless!

The Witness

Moreover He said to me: "Son of man, receive into your heart all My words that I speak to you, and hear with your ears. And go, get to the captives, to the children of your people, and speak to them and tell them, 'Thus says the Lord GOD,' whether they hear, or whether they refuse."

"Son of man, I have made you a watchman for the house of Israel; therefore hear a word from My mouth, and give them warning from Me: When I say to the wicked, 'You shall surely die,' and you give him no warning, nor speak to warn the wicked from his wicked way, to save his life, that same wicked *man* shall die in his iniquity; but his blood I will require at your hand. Yet, if you warn the wicked, and he does not turn from his wickedness, nor from his wicked way, he shall die in his iniquity; but you have delivered your soul."

"Again, when a righteous *man* turns from his righteousness and commits iniquity, and I lay a stumbling block before him, he shall die; because you did not give him warning, he shall die in his sin, and his righteousness which he has done

> shall not be remembered; but his blood I will require at your hand. Nevertheless, if you warn the righteous *man* that the righteous should not sin, and he does not sin, he shall surely live because he took warning; also you will have delivered your soul."
>
> —Ezek. 3:10-11, 17-21

Were you called to serve on a jury or have you been a witness in a criminal or murder case? I haven't, but I can only imagine the pressure and tension that builds inside that courtroom during the proceedings.

Imagine being on trial for murder and your best friend will have to testify against you. Imagine that your friend was the only witness in the case. How would your friendship hold up if he told the truth about what really happened? Would you still be friends afterward? Often, friends cover for friends, but I think in this type of situation, when the pressures are so high for both parties, the truth would have to come out. Would you remain friends after the truth came out and the jury convicted you of that crime?

Often, we Christians commit the same type of offense. What we don't realize is the world is our witness and it watches every step we make. It waits for us to stumble and fall. We need to switch roles and be a witness to the world. God will hold us accountable for the people we met but did not witness to during our time here on earth. We must put ourselves in the same situation the world is in because we were once lost and going to hell. When we get to heaven, we are accountable for not telling our family, friends, neighbors, or coworkers about Jesus. We won't be able to lie to Jesus as we stand before Him.

We need to step out of our front door, past that line we have drawn called our comfort zone, and go around our neighborhoods, knocking on doors to show others just how much Jesus cares about them. We need to be Jesus to the world. The world begins right outside our front door. You may feel uncomfortable doing this, but Jesus hung naked on the cross for our sins. That wasn't comfortable, either; however, He hung there and died so that He may shed His blood to cover our sins.

Get past your fear and start sharing the gospel. Help someone step from death into life and into a saving relationship with Jesus Christ. Don't be a gravedigger, be a life giver! God bless, and have a great day!

Three-Pointer

This is He who came by water and blood—Jesus Christ; not only by water, but by water and blood. And it is the Spirit who bears witness, because the Spirit is truth. For there are three that bear witness in heaven: the Father, the Word, and the Holy Spirit; and these three are one. And there are three that bear witness on earth: The Spirit, the water, and the blood; and these three agree as one.

If we receive the witness of men, the witness of God is greater; for this is the witness of God which He has testified of His Son. He who believes in the Son of God has the witness in himself; he who does not believe God has made Him a liar, because he has not believed the testimony that God has given of His Son. And this is the testimony: that God has given us eternal life, and this life is in His Son. He who has the Son has life; he who does not have the Son of God does not have life. These things I have written to you who believe in the name of the Son of God, that you may know that you have eternal life, and that you may *continue to* believe in the name of the Son of God.

—1 John 5:6-13

When most sport fans hear words like "three-pointer," they immediately think of basketball. You know what that means if you are a big fan of the game.

Since God saved me a little over three years, I, however, look at a three-pointer in a different way. I imagine a "three-pointer" as the points of the nails that crucified Christ on the cross—one in each hand and one in Jesus' feet. These three points saved my life and they can save yours. To me, each nail represents the death, the burial, and the resurrection. It is what Jesus went through for you and me. Jesus gave so much and we did nothing to deserve such a sacrifice. We are so unworthy of what He did on Calvary. Jesus showed us so much love by finishing what His Father sent Him to earth to do. Jesus went all the way for your sins and mine. He loved you and me so much that He died for us.

How can you receive the love and forgiveness that Jesus provided for us? All you have to do is ask Jesus to come into your life, forgive you of your sins, change you, and make you a new person. You must mean it with your whole heart. You can then begin a new life—a life that will never end. Go and tell everyone you see about the love of Jesus Christ. God bless, and have a great day!

Tightrope

Not that I have already attained, or am already perfected; but I press on, that I may lay hold of that for which Christ Jesus has also laid hold of me. Brethren, I do not count myself to have apprehended; but one thing I *do*, forgetting those things which are behind and reaching forward to those things which are ahead, press toward the goal for the prize of the upward call of God in Christ Jesus.

—Phil. 3:12-14

Most Christians go through life as if we are walking a tightrope. It is a balancing act that can lead to life or death. We walk such a thin wire between good and evil that sometimes we cannot distinguish between the two. Our lives are like the wire stretched between two destinations, one leading to our future and the other to our past. We are in the middle, surrounded by temptations, which is the world we live in.

The world is always trying to lead us in the wrong direction, trying to turn us around and head us back in the direction we once were. It seems the distance we traveled away from our sin is shorter than the distance to where God is leading us and wants us to be. However, the walk into our future looks like it will never end. We are tired of the battles we have to fight just to keep our balance. To press on to the future, we must keep our eyes and hearts focused on what is to come, and not what is behind us.

We need to keep our focus on the one thing that will keep us in a balanced fellowship with God. We can find that in Jesus Christ. We must have faith that Jesus will always be there to catch us if we fall. Jesus is our safety net. He will catch us and keep us from falling back into the hands of the world, the dominion of the evil ruler, Satan. Satan wants us back, but he can't have us, even though he tries to make us think we can lose our salvation. If that were the case, Jesus' death on the cross would have been in vain. We need to realize that Jesus' death was not in vain. We must believe this to have a successful walk. We must have a balanced diet of the Word of God and read all about God's promises. He will never break His promises. On the other hand, if you believe in the promises of the world, the world will knock you off balance every time. The world wants you to fall because it doesn't want you to have anything it doesn't have.

Don't be caught off balance. Trust in Jesus, and He will help you make it all the way to the other side! Have a great day!

Timetables

When then, *as* workers together *with Him* also plead with *you* not to receive the grace of God in vain. For He says:
"In an acceptable time I have heard you,
And in the day of salvation I have helped you."
Behold, now *is* the accepted time; behold, now *is* the day of salvation."

—2 Cor. 6:1-2

Everything in our lives is set on a timetable—a timetable of where we are supposed to be and when to get certain things done. Sometimes we allow this timetable to control our lives so much, that it can destroy our lives. We are always rushing to meet deadlines. Those tasks will still be there tomorrow if we do not accomplish them today. We rush around so much that we miss out on many opportunities.

Because of our selfishness, we miss opportunities God has planned for our lives. It is bad when we start putting a limit on the amount of time we spend with God. It is a sin if our time with God ends up being less than the time we spend doing other things—things we feel are more important than God is but are not going to help us in eternity. Timetables that control us become idols in our lives, and we begin to worship them more than the One who saved us through His Son, Jesus. We also limit the amount of time we spend with our families. This time is critical, especially for your marriage and children. If they do not get to spend time with you, they are going to find someone else to spend it with, and that person may not be someone you approve of. At least that person is willing to listen and willing to spend time with your child or with your spouse.

Marriage is another area we set timetables. When Jesus saves us, we become the bride of Christ, so this tells me that the union with our spouse is important and if it is important to God, it should be important to you. The time we spend together is less than the times we are apart. We need to reverse this deadly process, because if we do not shift around our time and priorities, we are heading for a disaster—one that could lead to the death of our marriage, the death of ourself, or even the death of our union with God. We know that God would never leave us nor forsake us, but what about us? Would we leave God and forsake Him? His timetable is not the same as ours. With the Lord, one day is as a thousand years, and a thousand years as one day (2 Peter 3:8).

Let us live as if Jesus is coming back at any second. If you have never repented of your sins and have asked Jesus to come live in your heart to save you and to change you as of this day, now is the time. What are you waiting for? Make this the day of your salvation. Remember, you do not know when Jesus will be returning. Only God knows His timetable. Have a great day, and God bless!

Transformed or Transplanted

And the word of the LORD came to me, saying, "Son of Man, pose a riddle, and speak a parable to the House of Israel, and say, 'Thus says the Lord GOD:

"A great eagle with large wings and long pinions,
Full of feathers of various colors,
Came to Lebanon
And took from the cedar the highest branch.
He cropped off its topmost young twig
And carried it to a land of trade;
He set it in a city of merchants.
Then he took some of the seed of the land
And planted it in a fertile field;
He placed *it* by abundant waters
And set it like a willow tree.
And it grew and became a spreading vine of low stature;
Its branches turned toward him,
But its roots were under it.
So it became a vine,

Brought forth branches,
And put forth shoots.
But there was another great eagle with large wings and many feathers;
And behold, this vine bent its roots toward him,
And stretched its branches toward him,
From the garden terrace where it had been planted,
That he might water it.
It was planted in good soil by many waters,
To bring forth branches, bear fruit,
And become a majestic vine.' "
"Say, 'Thus says the Lord GOD:
"Will it thrive?
Will he not pull up its roots,
Cut off its fruit,
And leave it to wither?
All of its spring leaves will wither,
And no great power or many people
Will be needed to pluck it up by its roots.
Behold, *it is* planted,
Will it thrive?
Will it not utterly wither when the east wind touches it?
It will wither in the garden terrace where it grew.' "

—Ezek. 17:1-10

With many Christians, life is kind of like a tree. They find a good church, which is rooted and grounded in the Word of God. Then they feed upon the Word, which in turn helps them grow. Then they plant themselves in a ministry which helps them branch out to help others grow. After that, they branch out and help some whose growth is stunted. Even with all this growth and transformation happening for their good, however, there is always someone or something in the thick of the woods that makes us fall like the season. It feels as if we lose everything, and joy drops off like the leaves on a tree. We feel naked, violated, and depressed, and we lay dormant for what seems like forever.

Then we begin blaming our fall on fellow Christians. We uproot ourselves from the fellowship in the woods and try to plant ourselves into another fellowship. What we do not realize is that every time we uproot ourselves, all the roots do not come up. Some are left behind, reminding others of what happened to us. When we try to plant ourselves in another fellowship with half of our roots missing, it makes it hard. The roots do not always take, so we uproot ourselves repeatedly. Every time we uproot, we leave roots behind, until finally we are very weak.

The only way we can survive is by the grace of God. Only God can heal and nurture us when our roots are so few and sow us back into fellowship so that we can grow again. Let us stay rooted in the Word, and let God handle your seasons. Have a blessed day!

Transmission

"I know your works, that you are neither cold nor hot. I could wish you were cold or hot. So then, because you are lukewarm, and neither cold nor hot, I will vomit you out of My mouth. Because you say, 'I am rich, have become wealthy, and have need of nothing'—and do not know that you are wretched, miserable, poor, blind, and naked—I counsel you to buy from Me gold refined in the fire, that you may be rich; and white garments, that you may be clothed, *that* the shame of your nakedness may not be revealed; and anoint your eyes with eye salve, that you may see. As many as I love, I rebuke and chasten. Therefore be zealous and repent.

—Rev. 3:15-19

Christians live their lives kind of like a car's transmission. Often, when we are saved, we never get out of park. We just sit there with our motors running, which is our mouths, telling everyone else what to do. We make loud noises with our engines because we want all of the attention. After we sit with our engines running for so long, we begin to sputter. Then we realize no one can understand a word we are sputtering. We sputter our last sputter and run out of gas. Our engines die.

Then you have the type of Christian who moves, but he moves in the wrong direction. He moves in reverse, because he has the mentality that he can keep on living as he lived before Jesus saved him. He is in reverse and keeps on sinning. He finally realizes he cannot live that way any longer. After he finds himself backed into a corner, he realizes that once you are backed into a corner, the only way to get out is to switch gears before it is too late.

The third type of Christian is a not any better than the last. He thinks he is better off, but he is actually in a worse gear than the reverse Christian. He has no gear. He is a neutral Christian. He thinks he is better off because he is in the middle; however, he can be switched into any gear at any time. It's kind of like riding the fence. You do not know what gear you want to slide into and most of the time it is the wrong gear. Don't slip into a gear that will get you into trouble.

The last Christian is a little better than the third one. At least he is moving in the right direction. He is in drive mode, but he is in the wrong seat. Have you ever seen the bumper sticker "God is my copilot?" It should read, "God is my pilot." Switch seats and let God in the driver seat, because His Son, Jesus, has the best driving record. He took the driving test when the nails were driven into His hands and feet. Jesus passed the test for us at Calvary.

Give God control of your transmission and let Him set the cruise control. He knows what gear it must be in to get you going in the right direction. Then, watch a transition take place in your life. Have a great day!

Trees

"Blessed is the man who trusts in the LORD,
And whose hope is the LORD.
For he shall be like a tree planted by the waters,
Which spreads out its roots by the river,
And will not fear when heat comes;
But its leaf will be green,
And will not be anxious in the year of drought,
Nor will cease from yielding fruit.

—Jer. 17:7-8

Have you ever cut down a tree or watched one cut down? Do you know that if you count the rings on the stump, you can tell how old the tree is? I have done this several times. It was amazing how old some of the trees were. I would have to count the rings several times to make sure I counted right. I have seen trees 100 to 200 years, and older—two to three times a person's life span! Of course, there are even older trees.

If you look at the center of the tree trunk, this is the heart of the tree. This is where it all began. The rings closest to the heart are pretty close together, but as the tree grows, season after season, the rings get farther apart or closer together, depending on how much rain has fallen during the year. If not much rain has fallen, the rings will be closer together, showing that not much growth has taken place. If a lot of rain has fallen, the rings will be farther apart, indicating more growth has occurred. Of course, there are other factors that affect growth, such as fire, insects, disease, and storms.

One can compare the life of a tree to the life of a Christian. You start out with your heart in the right place, but over the years, you go through different seasons. Your first couple of seasons might be great. You receive plenty of living water, which helps your spiritual growth. Your growth rings will be farther apart, showing everyone you had a good season. However, for every good season there is bound to be a dry one. This does not necessarily mean it is going to be a bad season. This could be the season to become stronger, meaning you have to dig deeper into the ground for the spring of living water, which places your roots deeper into the ground. This will allow you more stability for the next season or storm. However, if you give up during a dry season and do not search for anything to sustain your growth, you will become weak and lose stability. When the next storm or trial comes, you will be too weak and your roots will be so shallow that they cannot support the weight of your canopy full of your sin.

Therefore, next time you go through a wet season, which allows you to grow, be sure you keep your branches pruned of any dead or non-productive branches, so as you go through your next dry season, the weight of your branches will not weigh you down and cause you to fall. We must get rid of unrepented sin in our lives. Also, let us stay rooted in the Word of God so that we will be prepared for whatever season comes our way. God bless!

Tug-o-War

And one shall say,
"Heap it up! Heap it up!
Prepare the way,
Take the stumbling block out of the way of My people."
For thus says the High and Lofty One
Who inhabits eternity, whose name *is* Holy:
"I dwell in the high and holy *place*,
With him *who* has a contrite and humble spirit,
To revive the spirit of the humble,
And to revive the heart of the contrite ones.
For I will not contend forever,
Nor will I always be angry;
For the spirit would fail before Me,
And the souls *which* I have made.
For the iniquity of his covetousness
I was angry and struck him;
I hid and was angry,
And he went on backsliding in the way of his heart.

I have seen his ways, and will heal him;
I will also lead him,
And restore comforts to him
And to his mourners.
"I create the fruit of the lips:
Peace, peace to *him who is* far off and to *him who* is near,"
Says the LORD,
"And I will heal him."
But the wicked *are* like the troubled sea,
When it cannot rest,
Whose waters cast up mire and dirt.
"*There is* no peace,"
Says my God, "for the wicked."

—Isa. 57:14-21

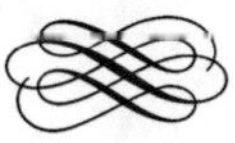

Life as a Christian can sometimes be like a game of tug-o-war between God and Satan. We are the flag in the middle. We are pulled one way, away from our sin, which is no problem for God to do as long as we trust Him and keep our eyes focused on Him. Because of our sinful nature, however, we often take our eyes off God. Once we take our eyes off God, we are pulled in the other direction, back into our sin. Then we fall into a pit, the world can sometimes be a living hell.

We must remember that Satan is real and he is constantly trying to pull us out of communion with God. Satan hates it when we are full of joy. His goal is to try to steal our joy by throwing things in our path to make us trip and fall back into our old sinful nature. Satan knows our past and hates our future, because the blood of Jesus Christ has sealed our future. Satan cannot have us back, even though he tries to convince us he can. He can pull and tug all he wants to. We may trip and fall, but God is faithful and will always pick us up and put us back in communion with Him.

Let us stop tugging on our past and let God pull us to our future. We do have a future and it's not of this world. Stay on your knees. It is hard to fall when you are on your knees—even harder when you are on your face. God bless, and have a great day!

Two-Minute Warning

It is better to trust in the LORD
Than to put confidence in man.

—Ps. 118:8

I think most men and some women like watching football or basketball. It is full of excitement and a lot of action. It consists of four quarters, each lasting fifteen minutes. A quarter can sometimes last forty-five minutes to an hour, because of all the timeouts and penalties that take place during the game. Then the game comes down to a two-minute warning. This is when you must make some critical decisions that will cause you either to win or lose the game.

Life is kind of like a ball game. If you think about it, life itself has four quarters. First, we are born as a baby. Then we move on to childhood, and from there we hit adolescence. From there we reach adulthood, and from that point, we live out the rest of our lives. During the first stage of our lives, we are fully dependant on someone to take care of us. We cannot do anything for ourselves. We can't feed ourselves, we can't walk until we are about one year old, we can't change our diapers or bathe ourselves. We must fully rely on someone else to meet our basic needs. As we go through childhood, we learn to take steps of independence. This is the age when we become more independent but we still need help in certain areas to survive. The biggest change in our lives takes place when we become teenagers. At this stage, we think we can take on the world by ourselves. We don't want to listen to our parents, we become more defiant toward those who love us most, and we make many wrong decisions that will stick with us the rest of our lives. Whether it is sex, alcohol, or drugs, we all make wrong decisions during this stage in our lives. Then we reach the pinnacle of our lives. When we become adults, we have usually moved away from home for various reasons, such as going to college, getting married and starting a family, or enlisting in the military. Whatever the reason, you are on your own and you are finally independent, or at least we think you are.

We all need somebody to look up to as a role model. These role models include people such as sports stars, movie stars, or big brother or sister. Unfortunately, there is a problem with this. There is the possibility that these people will eventually let you down. They are no different than you are: we all need somebody to depend on. I hate to break the news, but you won't find that person anywhere on earth, because He left about 2,000 years ago. However, He will be back! Before He left, He did something for us that no one on earth will ever do. He went to the cross on Calvary and died for your sins and mine, He did it all for love's sake.

Who is this man? His name is Jesus Christ. He loves you more than your own family and He wants to take you home with Him when He returns to earth one day. What do I have to do? Well, you first must get rid of your pride, and then humble yourself, ask Jesus to forgive you of your sins, and ask Him to come into your life, change you, and make you a new person. You also must believe in the death, burial, and resurrection of Jesus Christ.

Don't wait another minute! Time is running out! It's not a game; it's the difference between life and death. There isn't a two-minute warning but it has many penalties. So don't play games, because before you know it, your time will be up and the trumpet will sound. Will you be ready? I hope so. God bless, and heed the warning!

UFO

But I do not want you to be ignorant, brethren, concerning those who have fallen asleep, lest you sorrow as others who have no hope. For if we believe that Jesus died and rose again, even so God will bring with Him those who sleep in Jesus. For this we say to you by the word of the Lord, that we who are alive *and* remain until the coming of the Lord will by no means precede those who are asleep. For the Lord Himself will descend from heaven with a shout, and the voice of an archangel, and with the trumpet of God. And the dead in Christ will rise first. Then we who are alive *and* remain shall be caught up together with them in the clouds to meet the Lord in the air. And thus we shall always be with the Lord. Therefore comfort one another with these words.

—1 Thess. 4:13-18

Most people may say they have heard about or have witnessed an unidentified flying object (UFO) sighting. Millions of dollars are wasted each year on this research. I cannot believe there are people out there who believe in things from outer space or life that visits us from other planets. There are people who watch radar screens, listening for sounds, 24 hours a day and 7 days a week, that come from outer space.

There is only one person who came to this world from out of this world. He came from a heavenly place and His name is Jesus Christ. He came, He visited, and He died on a rugged cross for our sins. Then He ascended into heaven. He is now seated at the right hand of the Father. He will return to earth one day soon, and the researchers and their radars will finally hear something. It will sound like a trumpet blast, but some of them won't know what the sound means or where it came from. They never heard the Word of God, because they were too busy looking into space. Now, that space separates them from God.

When the trumpet sounds, will these researchers see millions of UFOs? If they do, will they still not understand? These UFOs will be the dead in Christ who are rising from their graves. Then the next wave of UFOs will be the living in Christ who will ascend into the clouds to meet Him in the air.

Sadly, some will still not understand. Christians must put on their spiritual radars and listen for the cries of the lost world. We must tell them so they will understand about Jesus and that He came into this world to save the lost souls of this world so we could spend eternity with Him. Have a great day and be a UFO!

Vegetable Garden

But He said to them, "I have food to eat of which you do not know."

Therefore the disciples said to one another, "Has anyone brought Him *anything* to eat?"

Jesus said to them, "My food is to do the will of Him who sent Me, and to finish His work.

Do you not say, 'There are still four months and *then* comes the harvest'? Behold, I say to you, lift up your eyes and look at the fields, for they are already white for harvest! And he who reaps receives wages, and gathers fruit for eternal life, that both he who sows and he who reaps may rejoice together. For in this the saying is true: 'One sows and another reaps.' I sent you to reap that for which you have not labored; others have labored, and you have entered into their labors."

—John 4:32-38

Have you ever planted a vegetable garden? It is a lot of work, no matter how big the garden is. It is a constant job tending to it. You have to weed it, cultivate it, spray it, prune it, and water it. It takes a lot of time and effort until it is time to harvest. Then you can eat the fruits of your labor.

If you compare the church to a garden, it's kind of the same principle. You reap what you sow. Unfortunately, most churches are full of more vegetables than fruits. Have you ever heard of a couch potato? The church is full of pew potatoes. Yes! They sit on their blessed spuds and do nothing but complain. They are full of ideas and there are plenty of eyes watching the 20 percent—which are the fruit—do 80 percent of the work.

So, are you a fruit or a vegetable? I hope you have more fruits than vegetables in the church you attend. Fruits are a lot sweeter than a bland potato, and fruits have more vitamin C. The vitamin C is what we have in Christ Jesus. The more you have, the more you sow and grow and, in turn, the more fruit you can harvest for the church.

Let us mash the potatoes and whip them into shape and start having them served more. God bless, and please pass the gravy!

Veneer

But there were also false prophets among the people, even as there will be false teachers among you, who will secretly bring in destructive heresies, even denying the Lord who bought them, *and* bring on themselves swift destruction. And many will follow their destructive ways, because of whom the way of truth will be blasphemed. By covetousness they will exploit you with deceptive words; for a long time their judgment has not been idle, and their destruction does not slumber.

For when they speak great swelling *words* of emptiness, they allure through the lusts of the flesh, through lewdness, the ones who have actually escaped from those who live in error. While they promise them liberty, they themselves are slaves of corruption; for by whom a person is overcome, by him also he is brought into bondage. For if, after they have escaped the pollutions of the world through the knowledge of the Lord and Savior Jesus Christ, they are again entangled in them and overcome, the latter end is worse for them than the beginning. For it would have been better for them not to have known the way of righteousness, than having known *it*, to turn from the holy commandment delivered to them. But it has happened to them according to the true proverb: "*A dog returns to his own vomit*," and, "a sow, having washed, to her wallowing in the mire."

—2 Peter 2:1-3, 18-22

We have all gone shopping for furniture at one time or another during our lives. Unfortunately, most of the time, what you see is not what you get. You have to look closely to be sure you are getting what you are paying for. Don't wait until you get home. Otherwise, you will find out what you thought you paid for is not what you got. Today, most often furniture is covered to make it appear to be something it's not. We see many furniture makers use what is called "veneer" to cover up a less expensive piece of wood to make it look like a more expensive one. Furniture stores are so big and so full of many types of furniture that we become overwhelmed at all the choices we have. By the time we make a decision, we are so tired of looking at all the furniture that we end up making the wrong choice.

The world is the same way. People also cover things with veneer. They intend to blind us and make us see things for what they really are not. They do this to attract us to things we have no business getting involved in from the beginning. They make things so enticing with the false veneers that our flesh takes control and we end up falling into sin. When Christians are saved, we are supposed to release everything to Jesus when He comes into our lives. However, we often bring the veneers we had in the flesh with us into our Christian walk. Then we wonder why we are not growing closer to God. Instead of growing closer, our growth is stunted because of all the veneers we still have. When we are saved, the veneers we carried into our Christian life tell God we do not trust Him fully. We have no reason not to trust God fully because He sent His Son, Jesus, into the world to save it, not to condemn it (John 3:17). Jesus died on a rugged cross for my sins and the sins of the world. He did it out of love for you and me. The cross Jesus died on was real. It wasn't covered with veneer to make it look like something it wasn't. It was the real deal. There was nothing to hide. However, our sins needed to be covered—not with the veneers in our lives but with the blood Jesus shed on the cross on Calvary. We need to let God strip us of our veneers and let Him expose us for what we really are. Then God can begin to work in us and through us.

So, don't be something you're not. Be what God intended you to be and stop fooling yourself, because you cannot fool God. Have a great day, and God bless!

Weapons of Mass Destruction

And who *is* he who will harm you if you become followers of what is good? But even if you should suffer for righteousness' sake, *you are* blessed. "*And do not be afraid of their threats, nor be troubled.*" But sanctify the Lord God in your hearts, and always *be* ready to *give* a defense to everyone who asks you a reason for the hope that is in you, with meekness and fear; having a good conscience, that when they defame you as evildoers, those who revile your good conduct in Christ may be ashamed. For *it is* better, if it is the will of God, to suffer for doing good than for doing evil.

—1 Peter 3:13-17

I don't know about you, but I am sure tired of hearing about this war in Iraq and that no weapons of mass destruction have been found. Unfortunately, if you think about it, we ourselves are letting more people die and go to hell than any weapon of mass destruction ever killed. You may be wondering how I came to that conclusion. Well, all you have to do is look around at the people in your family and those with whom you work and associate. We need to tell people about salvation and how they can have a relationship with Jesus Christ, or they will all be going to hell.

I don't know about you, but I don't want to be held accountable for their deaths. Why would you or I be held accountable? If you read Matthew 28:19 it says, "Go ye therefore and teach all nations baptizing them in the name of the Father and of the Son and the Holy Ghost." "How can I reach all these people by myself?" you ask. Well, if you take one soul at a time and start a fire in one person's life, then that person can go out and ignite a fire in someone else's. You may feel uncomfortable witnessing or sharing your faith with family and friends. What is easier—telling a friend or a coworker about Jesus or being held accountable the day you meet Jesus face to face? Jesus will ask you why you didn't tell more people about Him. What are you going to say to the One who knows everything about you? You can't hide anything from the One who created you.

Let us not miss another opportunity to tell someone about the One who can change his or her destiny forever. That one person is Jesus Christ. Do not be a weapon of mass destruction. Be a witness of mass construction and build up the kingdom of God. Have a great day! Reach out and touch someone in Jesus' name. Amen!

Wedding Invitation

"But of that day and hour no one knows, not even the angels in heaven, nor the Son, but only the Father. Take heed, watch and pray; for you do not know when the time is. *It is* like a man going to a far country, who left his house and gave authority to his servants, and to each his work, and commanded the doorkeeper to watch. Watch therefore, for you do not know when the master of the house is coming—in the evening, at midnight, at the crowing of the rooster, or in the morning—lest, coming suddenly, he find you sleeping. And what I say to you, I say to all: Watch!"

—Mark 13:32-37

I think one of the biggest days in a person's life is their wedding day. Next to having a baby, it is a very special day. It's getting to that special day that will drive you crazy. When you begin planning your wedding, you cannot wait for the big day to arrive so that you can start your new life together. However, it is that time getting to the big day that will change your outlook. You may start thinking, "I can't wait until this day is over." Everyone wants to help and give advice on wedding invitations, who should make the cake, where you should hold the reception, how many people you should invite, and whom you should invite. By the time the wedding day is here, you are so stressed that it is hard to enjoy your special day. When all is said and done, you have lost your best friend and family members are no longer talking to one another. You received three mixers as wedding gifts. You have to return them to the local department store, but the people who bought the mixers work at the store and see you returning their gifts.

Aren't you glad you have a friend in Jesus? He is planning your future wedding day. There will be no gifts to buy or return. All He asks is that you receive His gift of salvation by repenting of your sins, asking Him to be your personal Lord and Savior, and asking Him to come into your heart and change you. It is free and it's one of a kind.

Then, all Jesus asks you to do is send out invitations to invite people into His kingdom. Invite them by telling them how much Jesus loves them and what He did on Calvary for you. "For God so love the world that He gave His only begotten Son, that whoever believes in Him shall not perish, but shall have everlasting life (John 3:16)." That wedding day has been planned. The day and the time has already been predetermined, but we do not know when that will be, nor does Jesus.

When the big day comes, are you going to be ready? All you have to do is receive the gift of life that Jesus Christ provides.

Windshields

"Therefore say to the house of Israel, 'Thus says the Lord GOD: "I do not do *this* for your sake, O house of Israel, but for My holy name's sake, which you have profaned among the nations wherever you went. And I will sanctify My great name, which has been profaned among the nations, which you have profaned in their midst; and the nations shall know that I *am* the LORD," says the Lord GOD, "when I am hallowed in you before their eyes. For I will take you from among the nations, gather you out of all countries, and bring you into your own land. Then I will sprinkle clean water on you, and you shall be clean; I will cleanse you from all your filthiness and from all your idols. I will give you a new heart and put a new spirit within you; I will take the heart of stone out of your flesh and give you a heart of flesh. I will put My Spirit within you and cause you to walk in My statutes, and you will keep My judgments and do *them*. Then you shall dwell in the land that I gave to your fathers; you shall be My people, and I will be your God. I will deliver you from all your uncleannesses. I will call for the grain and multiply it, and bring no famine upon you. And I will multiply the fruit of your trees and the increase of your fields, so that you need never again bear the reproach of famine among the nations. Then you will remember your evil ways and your deeds that *were* not good; and you will loathe yourselves in your own sight, for your iniquities and your abominations. Not for your sake do I do *this*," says the Lord GOD, "let it be known to you. Be ashamed and confounded for your own ways, O house of Israel!"

—Ezek. 36:22-32

When we start out in life, we have a pretty clear view of it. It's like looking through a clean windshield as we drive down the road of life. The more driving we do, the more we realize that our lives are not as clear as the view we had when we started out. As the view becomes more clouded, it is harder to see our destination, and often we miss it and end up in the wrong place at the wrong time. We end up getting more dirt splattered on our windshields. We then try to wipe away the dirt, which is the sin we have accumulated during our lifetime, off our windshields, but we end up smearing it even more. Then our vision really becomes impaired. We start trusting people we should not and believe what they say, instead of what we perceive. It's kind of like listening to something you didn't witness, but you believe it, anyway.

That is how a rumor gets started. We must stop listening and start witnessing, but that is impossible with all the sin we have on our life's windshield. We need to search for the hope, which is the rain shower we find in Jesus Christ. Jesus showed us His love on the cross on Calvary. He showed it by shedding His blood for our sins and the sins of the world. The blood He shed will cleanse us of the sins we have accumulated on our windshields and will make it so we can see clearly again. Jesus came to die on the cross for our sins and rose from the dead three days later. When He ascended into heaven to be with His Father, He sent us the Holy Spirit in His place to comfort us and keep us on the right road until His return.

I know life is not going to be easy. If we do happen to travel down the wrong road, however, the Holy Spirit will be there to convict us of our wrongs, and if we listen to the Spirit, we will then turn around and ask Jesus to forgive us. Look at the Holy Spirit as being the water that washes our windshield and Jesus as the windshield wipers that wipe our sins away. Don't forget to fill up daily with the Word of God, to replenish the Spirit within us. Have a great day and keep your windshields spotless! God bless!

Wood, Hay & Stubble

> "Therefore whoever hears these sayings of Mine, and does them, *I* will liken him to a wise man who built his house on the rock: and the rain descended, the floods came, and the winds blew and beat on that house; and it did not fall, for it was founded on the rock."
>
> "But everyone who hears these sayings of Mine, and does not do them, will be like a foolish man who built his house on the sand: and the rain descended, the floods came, and the winds blew and beat on that house; and it fell. And great was its fall."
>
> —Matt. 7:24-27

Once upon a time, there were three brothers who lived in a small town north of the Red Sea in a small fishing village. The brothers were great fishermen and great navigators of the sea. They were strong physically, but only one was strong spiritually. This man believed that Jesus came into this world to die on the cross for his sins and the sins of the world. He believed that Jesus was buried and rose from the dead three days later, and then ascended to heaven, and now is seated at the right hand of His Father. The three brothers go through life fishing, making good money at their trade. Unfortunately, two of them wasted their money on expensive wine and sexual pleasures. Often, the two were broke, came to work drunk, and became so very lazy that they began depending on the responsible brother to take care of them.

Meanwhile, the oldest brother invested his money in the church he attended. He believed that all the money belonged to God, anyway, and knew God could do more with 10 percent (tithe) than he could do with the other 90 percent.

A time came when the two brothers needed a place to live, but they didn't have the money to build a decent house, so they used what they could find. The first brother found a farmer baling straw, and with the little money he had, he bought several bales of straw to build a shelter to live in. It wasn't much, but it kept him out of the weather.

The second brother found a carpenter and asked him if he could take the scraps of wood to build a shelter. The man felt sorry for him and gave him the wood.

The third brother, who trusted God, was able to build a house big enough for all three brothers. He built his house on the rock. As the months passed, the two brothers who wasted their money could not afford to run their business anymore, so the oldest brother bought their fishing fleets and tripled his fleet. This made the two brothers happy that they didn't have the responsibility of running their fleets anymore. The one brother paid them well for their fishing businesses, but he knew the money they received wouldn't last very long.

A few more months went by and, just as he thought, the two brothers were broke once again. One night a storm blew through the small fishing town. The two brothers rushed home to seek shelter from the storm. When the first brother arrived home, however, there was nothing left. The storm had ravaged his home. That brother then rushed to the second brother's house and found it still standing. He knocked on the door and his brother invited him in as he told his brother what had happened. The two brothers began to drink again and drank until they passed out. The storm raged on through the night. When the brothers awoke from the sun beating down on them, they realized the storm had taken everything they had. They had nowhere to go. They were lost and homeless.

The one brother whom they thought hated them because of the way they lived had been out all night looking for them to bring them home with him. That brother's house had withstood the storm because he had built his house on a firm foundation and had put his faith and trust in God. He invited his two brothers to live with him and gave them a new lease on life, just as Jesus had done for him many years ago. The three brothers worked together and the two who didn't know about Jesus learned about Him through their brother's actions and became believers themselves.

Have a great day! Begin trusting God through all the storms in your life and build your life on a firm foundation, which is in Jesus Christ!

Scripture References

Inside Out...1 Samuel 16:6-7
Junk Collector...Psalm 25:16-18
Level ....Matthew 7:13-14
Life Insurance...Ephesians 1:11-14
Life or Death Sentence.......................... Revelations 20:11-15
Life's a Beach .... Isaiah 1:16,18
Life's Signs .... Luke 21:25-28
Limited Time Offer..................................... Hebrews 3:12-19
Love Letter to God .... Romans 8:31-39
MIA... Hebrews 6:9-12
Magnetism .... Galatians 5:16-18
Mailbox of Sin... Jeremiah 17:9-10
Mapping it Out.. Jeremiah 29:11-13
Most Wanted.. Romans 10:8-13
Nails..Colossians 2:13-15
New Owner ....Ephesians 4:17-24
No Respect..Philippians 2:1-11
POW...1 John 2:15-17
Past Due.. 1 Corinthians 3:6-15
Piñata.. Mark 7:14-23
Polygraph Test ....Psalm 139:1-6
Real or Make Believe.......................................Isaiah 44:6-8
Recyclable Soul ....Matthew 5:13-16
Remote Control ....Matthew 1:18-25
Rent-a-Sinner..Psalm 55:16-18
Retread..Proverbs 14:14-15
Return to Sender..James 4:1-4
Reverse Interrogation .... Luke 16:22-31
Riding the Fence ....Philippians 2:12-16
River ....Psalm 39:4-6
Road Trip ....Proverbs 4:25-27
Rodeo ....Psalm 37:39-40
Rumor Seeds ....Proverbs 26:20-25, 28
Scanners..Psalm 19:7-14

Pleasant
Word

Printed in the United States
68858LVS00002B/61-66

9 781414 107615